The

PATRON SAINT

OF

USED CARS

and

SECOND CHANCES

The
PATRON SAINT
OF
USED CARS
and
SECOND CHANCES

A Memoir

MARK MILLHONE

RODALE

Rodale books may be purchased for business or promotional use or for special sales. For information, please write to:

Special Markets Department, Rodale Inc., 733 Third Avenue, New York, NY 10017

Printed in the United States of America

Rodale Inc. makes every effort to use acid-free ∞, recycled paper ♺.

Book design by Christopher Rhoads

Library of Congress Cataloging-in-Publication Data

Milhone, Mark.
  The patron saint of used cars and second chances : a memoir / Mark Milhone.
    p. cm.
  ISBN-13 978-1-59486-823-8 hardcover
  ISBN-10 1-59486-823-9 hardcover
  1. Milhone, Mark—Family.   2. Husbands—United States—Biography.
  3. Fathers—United States—Biography.   4. Marriage—Humor.   I. Title.
  HQ756.M55   2009
  306.874'2092—dc22
  [B]   2008051728

Distributed to the trade by Macmillan

2   4   6   8   10   9   7   5   3   1   hardcover

We inspire and enable people to improve their lives and the world around them

For more of our products visit **rodalestore.com** or call 800-848-4735

for my family

CONTENTS

PROLOGUE: THE YEAR FROM HELL

MY WIFE AND I had an open marriage. Rose understood that I had certain automotive needs, and I didn't ask questions about all the strange shoes she brought home. For me, eBayMotors was like online porn you could talk about around the water cooler the next day. My kink was grandma cars. Cars driven only by little old ladies to church on Sundays. Cherry. Mint as new money. Like new. That's what I'm talking about. Every car starts off new, like a baby, but only cars that the fates have smiled upon, to whom life has been truly kind, can remain *like new*, ever young, untouched by the ravages of time.

My obsession with finding this Platonic ideal of a used car on eBay began after a year from hell put far too many miles on my family: Our youngest, Benny, nearly died because of birth complications, my father was diagnosed with prostate cancer, my mother had a heart attack and passed away, and, finally, our family dog gave our older son, Sam, an object lesson in why you let sleeping dogs lie in the form of a jagged two-inch scar down the center of his face. It averaged out to a major crisis every five weeks or so, almost like a subscription to a tragedy-of-the-month club.

We want to think of crisis as a thing that brings us together. And most do—for as long as the crisis lasts. When things are reduced to life and death, it's much easier to know who you are, what you should do, what life means. There's a certain painful magic to it. And it's true what they say about crisis showing you what you're really made of; what they don't tell you is that you may not always like what you find out. Or that it's after the worst is over that the fun really begins.

Post-traumatic stress: the gift that keeps on taking.

I just kept telling myself we were "fine." So Rose was having a few issues. Nothing to get excited about, just your run-of-the-mill post-traumatic stuff: difficulty sleeping, panic attacks, agoraphobia, killer migraines, whiplash mood swings, that sort of thing. But the kids were fine. I mean, Benny was having some speech delays because of his time in the Neonatal Intensive Care Unit, but we were *pretty sure* there wasn't any irreversible neurological damage. And yes, Sam's nose scar was still quite noticeable a year after the dog bite, but that was no biggie because who was lucky enough to know the best plastic surgeon in the city? That's right, *us*. Why wait for puberty to make him self-conscious about his scar when we could have a crack medical team poke and prod him next Thursday at one o'clock?

Anybody who tells you that denial isn't a real way of dealing with things has never had to deal with anything real.

Soon after our troubles started, an uninvited houseguest showed up in our home. He ate my food, wore my clothes, played with my children, and even slept with my wife. He was my spitting image, but he wasn't me—at least not the "me" my wife had fallen in love with. I had become my father. My family needed me to be strong, and the only indelible image of manhood I had was that of my father, a classic '50s model: stoic, rational, dutiful, physically present but emotionally absent. Somebody had to wear the daddy pants.

As an angry young man, I had been quite adept at telling my father to go to hell. But now that the shoe was on the other foot, now that I was the dad, it was very hard for me to banish our uninvited houseguest, this emotionally withdrawn stranger that I had become. He saved my life. There's no way I could have soldiered through our year from hell without his quiet strength.

In family pictures taken in the wake of our year from hell, Rose and I actually have the thousand-yard stare of young soldiers made old by combat. Post-traumatic stress turns your world upside down: When the end of the world becomes your comfort zone, each new crisis is actually a relief—from the stress of worrying about what will befall you next, from all the difficult emotions that threaten to overwhelm you whenever you get a quiet moment to yourself. Just because you're not making time for your feelings doesn't mean they take the hint and go away.

When life-and-death conflicts become routine, routine conflicts become life-and-death. Who should leave work early to pick up the kids, whose fault it was the DVDs never made it back to the video store, which in-laws got which holidays—all became fights to the death. Arguing became the new sex. We could get it on anywhere, anytime, even in public places; we'd have shouting matches in the street. Yeah, we became *those* people. Even though the only real explanation for what happened to us was just the fine print about life not being fair, when bad things happen, you want someone, something, to blame. God wasn't returning our calls, so we turned on each other.

Me vs. my wife had always been a pretty fair fight. Rose is the irresistible force to my unmovable object—she attacks with the ear-biting, guilt-tripping ferocity of a Jewish Mike Tyson, while my tactic is to slowly wear her down with my passive-aggressive rope-a-dope like some corn-fed Muhammad Ali.

The brutal elegance of the passive-aggressive way is that you make your enemies fight themselves. Rose, with all her Jewish guilt, never stood a chance. I would attack at night, wielding my laptop with the devastating force of Bruce Lee spinning his nunchucks. Rose would wake to find that I had left our bed. All she could hear were my fingers on my laptop:

Clickity-clack . . . clickity clack . . .

Her insomnia would tag-team with her guilt, torturing her for hours—was I up late working because taking care of the kids during the day didn't leave me enough time to get my work done? Or was I on some porn site to make up for our nonexistent sex life? Was she a bad mother or a bad wife? Both?

Clickity-clack . . . clickity clack . . .

Most nights, I was just on eBay.

eBay accepted me the way I was. All I needed to feel adequate was my laptop and a PayPal account. To avoid that last argument of the day, I would generously offer to get Benny down to sleep each night, snuggling up with him and my laptop until he—and, more importantly, Rose—went to sleep.

It was on one of these nights that I found THE car:

eBAY LISTING #4620111528: LOW, LOW, LOW MILES—
Amazing 1994 BMW 740i in Orient Blue Metallic over Parch-
ment Leather. An absolutely impeccable example of a truly
fine luxury car . . .

It was a one-owner car kept in a climate-controlled garage in Dallas for the CEO of a large corporation in case he ever felt like driving himself to the golf course when he was in town. Never driven in the snow. Never smoked in. Never crashed.

Like new.

I know—it takes a *real man* to think that the answer to all our problems was buying a car. I spent hours staring at the twenty-three pictures of it posted online until I knew every inch of it, could almost feel the steering wheel in my hands. It was more than car lust, more than early-onset midlife crisis—this car became my Holy Grail, my *Field of Dreams,* my prayer to Saint eBay, patron saint of used cars and second chances, that my family could emerge from our time of trial like new. What happened to that brave couple Rose and I used to be, who wagered our lives on the fleeting magic of our first kiss? How could I find my way back to them? As I stared at this car on eBay, a voice in my head told me:

"If you drive it, you will know."

Chapter One

NEW YORK

"**Y**OU DID *WHAT*?" Rose said when I told her about the car.

Her brow seemed perpetually furrowed now, even in sleep—her cute freckle-face a mass of wrinkles in the making. She tucked a lock of hair, gone white at the roots, behind one ear, watching me, bird-intense, glasses askew like she'd been punched, as I stalled for time before answering her question. *When did she get so thin?*

Rose had gained so much weight during her last pregnancy that I had made peace with the idea of being the guy with the fat wife. I sincerely missed my fat wife. Not only did the plus-size Rose seem more healthy than the scarecrow with whom I now shared my bed, I also thought that having a fat wife would confer upon me a substance of an extra-physical sort; people would assume that I was a man of character, who cared about the things that really mattered in life. Alas, Rose had disappointed me by dropping seventy-five pounds, seemingly overnight, without ever once resorting to physical exercise. She liked to joke that our year from hell had saved her the price of a gym membership. Nothing like personal tragedy to really attack those thighs. A strict diet of Coca-Cola and migraine pills didn't hurt either. Rose took one while I was talking to her.

"Is it a bad one?" I asked.

"I feel like someone is stabbing my right eye. The usual. I'm sorry, you were saying something?"

"I found you a new car."

"Me? I don't drive."

"But don't you remember that road trip up to your folks' place over the holidays when you said our car wasn't big enough for the two of us, let alone the kids?"

"That had nothing to do with the car."

I sighed. "Well, since you're stuck with me, I thought maybe a bigger car would help." She slowly shook her head, giving me ample time to ponder which part of my statement was false—the part about the car or the part about being stuck with me. It had come to my attention that Rose viewed the rest of her life as a husband-optional event. Little signs like taking off her wedding ring and slamming it down on my desk.

"Why don't you just admit that *you* want the car?" Rose finally said, taking a sip of Coke and cranking up her laptop. Our bed was always strewn with her work, making going to sleep like curling up on her desk.

"Fine. I want the car."

"Thank you. Too bad we can't afford it."

"Well . . . technically I already bought it. I won the auction on eBay last night." I braced for her counterattack, but she just rolled her eyes. Was I so predictable? When had I lost my ability to surprise this woman? To surprise myself, for that matter?

"What's so special about this car?"

"It's, um . . . well . . . it's kind of this *Field of Dreams* thing. It's like it's calling to me. I can't explain it, but I have to have it."

Rose nodded, pretending to take me seriously, and then said, "You need help."

"Thanks."

"I mean it. You have a problem."

"Thank you, Imelda Marcos."

"Hey, I will wear *all* those shoes."

"Uh-huh."

"I *will*."

I felt sorry for my wife's shoe collection. Imagine the life of Cinderella's glass slippers if Cinderella never went to the ball. The world had proven a dangerous place of late, and more and more Rose ventured out less and less. She rarely left our bedroom. Even the living room seemed hostile territory, under siege by my insurgent home-improvement projects. She still had an office, a nice one, with two assistants—whom, I imagined, felt as abandoned as her shoe collection now that Rose worked almost exclusively from home, running her pocket business empire from her bed, in her pajamas. Like Hugh Hefner but without the fun. Rose said she liked to work from home, but still, I felt for those beautiful shoes of hers. There was something heartbreaking about all of them lined up in her closet like soldiers at parade rest, waiting for Rose to get all dressed up, but there was no place to go. No place Rose felt comfortable. I tried to see her recent return to shopping as a hopeful sign—she was starting to accessorize for her return to a life where all she had to worry about was what to wear.

"Well, I'll drive this car, too," I said.

"Whatever."

"It will only take a few days to go get it."

"A few *days*? Where is it?"

"Dallas. I thought I would see if I could talk my dad into flying down with me so we could drive it back together, have some father-son time."

"Since when do you and your dad have father-son time?"

"I think he's lonely without Mom. This trip could take his mind off things."

"But what about your work? What about all the renovations here on the apartment? What about the kids? You're just going to take off and leave me to deal with all that? This is making my headache worse." She turned away from me, a hand over her right eye, almost as if I was the one stabbing her there.

"I'm sorry. I know it's a bad time for you," I said.

"It's always a bad time lately."

"I'll take care of everything. Trust me."

"But what if something happens?!"

"Something like what?"

"Like . . ." she said, her voice trailing off. Her face twitched and I could tell she was filling in that blank with all the "somethings" that had already befallen us *and* a detailed list of all the new potential "somethings" that kept her up nights worrying. Rose was nothing if not thorough.

The phone rang, the sudden noise making her flinch.

"Leave me alone!" she yelled at the phone or at me or at her headache or at the world.

"This is Rose," she said, startlingly calm as she answered the phone. Her ability to juggle her work with her ongoing nervous breakdown truly amazed. She was our family's primary breadwinner. Compared to her, the money I brought in as an itinerant writer and college professor was the occasional bake sale. "No, this is a *perfect* time, just a sec." She covered the phone and then turned to me. "Don't you dare do anything about this car without talking to Sam first."

"Great idea!" I said, turning to walk out of our room. While I knew that *"Don't do anything without talking to Sam first"* was miles away from an agreement, it was within shouting distance of plausible deniability as long as I could get Sam to go along. He was the linchpin. A lot of pressure for your average kindergartener, but he could take it.

Our year from hell had made Sam old beyond his years. After the first Christmas without my mom, a Christmas of too many presents to make up for the emptiness in my parents' house, I was walking Sam to preschool when he cleared his throat and announced, "Dad, I want to go live with Grandpa John."

"Well . . . we can sure go visit him again soon."

"No, Dad—I want to *live* with Grandpa John."

"Um, okay . . . why?" I said, kneeling down to look into his wide-set gold-green eyes, the color of leaves turning.

"Well, now that Grandma Carole's gone, he's really all by himself."

I hugged him. That he would have the ability, at his tender age, to look beyond his own sadness in this way . . . I was in awe. Nothing can make you more proud as a father—or more humble—than having a four-year-old who's a bigger man than you are.

SAM WAS NOW SIX years old, his brother Benny, two and a half. I gathered them around the kitchen table, ants-in-my-pants giddy about showing them pictures of our new car on my laptop. Even Spike, our French bulldog, was barking, excited. Spike had a hoarse little bark that sounded like an old man coughing. I wish I could say I found it charming. A year after getting the little beast, I was still waiting for it to grow on me. Its round, feline head and gravity-defying ears made Spike look like Frankenstein tried to whip up a dog using leftover cat parts.

"See, it's a BMW just like Speedy, but it's got a V8 engine so it can go really, really fast," I said, pointing to the pictures on eBay.

"Faster than Speedy?" Sam asked. He had named our current car (*another* low-mileage used BMW I had found on eBay) "Speedy," after the cartoon character Speedy Gonzales because he thought it was the fastest car in the world. (Sam, as the oldest, had jurisdiction over the naming of all cars and pets, at least until Benny got old enough to get wind of this.) Speedy Gonzales was a dark green 1998 5 series. The "new" used BMW was a 1994 7 series and had a bigger engine. "Yep, faster than Speedy," I said.

"But nothing's faster than Speedy!"

"Okay, it's *as fast* as Speedy, and it has more room for when we go on a long drive."

"Cool!" Sam said.

"C-c-c-aaarrr . . . " Benny struggled to get out.

"That's right, Benny! *Car!*"

Benny beamed. He has my father's blue eyes and a smile so infectious it's almost physically impossible to frown in his presence. Every time he said a new word, we would praise him to the moon. Now two, he was still hunting and pecking for words at an age when Sam had been speaking in complete sentences. This speech delay and a scar on the right side of his chest where doctors had inserted a tube to reinflate a collapsed lung were Benny's souvenirs from spending the first two weeks of his life in the Neonatal Intensive Care Unit. He pulled that chest tube out three times. While this dramatically demonstrated his will to live, it had the unfortunate side effect of almost killing him. For better or worse, Benny had inherited the stubbornness gene from both his parents.

"This is *so* awesome," Sam said, looking at the car on eBay. "Mommy, now we're going to have *two* cars!" Sam said.

"No, we're *not*," Rose said.

"But . . . what's going to happen to Speedy?"

"Well, I've been talking to a friend of mine, and her family could really use a good car like Speedy."

"You're going to sell Speedy?" Sam looked at me in open-mouthed horror and then started to bawl as if I'd just told him I was going to sell *Benny* to another family. I looked up at Rose.

"You're on your own. You broke him, you fix him," she said.

I looked at Sam. His face gets all smooshed up when he cries, which just accentuates his scar from the dog bite. It makes the line of pink scar tissue running down the center of his nose glow bright red, like blowing on hot coals. Each new pain just seems to add heat to the old injury.

Benny pointed at Sam, concerned.

"Sa-sa . . . Sa-sa!"

"Don't worry, Benny. Sa-sa's going to be okay."

I tried to hug Sam, but he pushed me away. Of course, to Sam, Speedy *was* like a member of our family—he had named him. There was nothing wrong with Speedy except for the memory of too many weekend getaways that got us nowhere but someplace new and different to have the same old issues. Speedy wasn't *like new* anymore.

"Sam, listen to me. I didn't want to make you sad. I know this would be a change, but change can be good. Change is . . . is life, and if we don't embrace change, then it's . . . it's like saying *no thank you* to life. It's like giving life a *timeout.* And you don't want to give life a timeout, because if you do, then maybe life will give *you* a timeout."

Sam stared at me like I had three heads, trying to make sense of what I said. I didn't know if this line of bull was going to work for him, but I had myself half-sold—say yes to change, yes to life!

"You mean, if we don't get the new car, I'm going to be in timeout *for the rest of my life*?!" Sam yelped and collapsed on the floor in a puddle of his own tears. I picked him up and hugged him tight, shaking my head.

"Sam," I said. "Sam, I'm sorry." *I'm sorry that your old man is a selfish bastard who thought only about himself.* I knew at this moment that my firm belief that I could never mess up my kids the way my folks messed up me was a hundred percent correct: I could be worse.

I called the eBay seller, a BMW dealer down in Dallas, and gave him the *Reader's Digest* version of our tale of woe to beg out of my commitment to buy the car. The used-car salesman, Bill, just made the whole thing worse by being awfully, terrifically nice about it.

"I'm not worried about selling the car. This car sells itself. It's a honey. Just too bad because it seemed like you really wanted it, and as a salesman, that's what I take pleasure in—finding the right car for the right person."

"You don't talk like a used-car salesman."

"Well, I'm also a deacon in my church. I don't think of the jobs as being all that different. Just helping people get where they need to go in life."

I hung up the phone and went to Rose's fortress of solitude to tell her the news.

"I'm not getting the car."

"Really?" Rose said, looking up from her laptop.

"Why is that a surprise? You saw how Sam was."

"Well, I know, but it seemed like you really wanted it."

"And you thought I would choose a car over my kid, thanks a lot."

"I didn't say that."

"You implied it."

She shook her head. "I *knew* that if this didn't work out, you were going to figure out some way to make me feel bad."

"I didn't say I blamed you for anything!"

"Well, I guess you just *implied* it then."

Touché.

"I'm sorry I got so crazy about that car," I said. "I really thought I was *supposed* to have it . . . for some reason. It just felt . . . " I shook

my head. "It was dumb. I've wasted enough time on it. It was just .
silly. Maybe that was the whole point, I don't know . . . "

"What?" Rose asked.

"Just to do something silly."

"That's . . . silly."

"Well, we used to do a lot of silly things. We bought that old
farmhouse together, before we were married, even. Bought it sight
unseen. That was—"

"Romantic?"

"I was going to say fun. We used to be fun."

We both smiled, but sadly, like we were remembering good
friends who'd passed on. We had become that special kind of strangers, the kind who know each other only too well. The kind you
want to think only lived in other people's houses, in other people's
unhappy marriages. We lived around each other, separated by the
morning paper at breakfast and by everything that had happened
to us when we went to bed each night.

I wanted us to be like those people you see on talk shows who
emerge from adversity chock-full of *carpe diem*, ready to jog across
America on one leg because they're just so darn happy to be alive.
Instead, I lay awake nights wishing I were dead, blaming myself for
Sam's dog bite. Rose kept me company on these long, sleepless
nights, surfing the Web for what *she* must have done during her
pregnancy to give Ben the life-threatening pneumonia with which
he had been born. Our nightly *ménage à trois* with guilt. It was
easier to blame ourselves—or, better yet, each other!—than face the
fact that these things, these terrible things, can and do *just happen*;
that we live in a world where death can fall from a clear blue sky,
and there is nothing we can do to completely protect our children.

"THE BLUE BECKHAM BOMBER," Rose said the next night after I came back from taking Spike for one of our endless walks only to have her come back and "go makey" in the house.

"The what?" I said, stooping to clean up the mess.

"The Blue Beckham Bomber, that's what Sam says we should call it."

"Call what?"

"The car. Your effort to manipulate him was totally off. You don't get what you want from a six-year-old that way. You have to *bribe* him, silly."

I shook my head in wonder. "So, what's this going to cost me?"

"A day trip for you and Sam to the National Soccer Hall of Fame while wearing full David Beckham regalia, followed by a Happy Meal dinner at McDonald's and, of course, the naming rights to the car as previously stipulated—the Blue Beckham Bomber."

"That's it?"

"I have one nonnegotiable condition—if any of this interferes with finishing the renovations to put in the central air, I'll kill you. With my asthma, I won't make it through another summer in this place without it."

"Thanks, honey."

"For threatening to kill you?"

"For trying to make me happy."

"You sound surprised."

"I am, a little."

I hugged her. It had been so long since I held Rose that it felt like cheating. But this strange woman in whose arms I found myself was my wife. It was funny at first, then terribly, terribly sad—to physically feel how far apart we'd grown. Rose wriggled free.

I CALLED MY DAD TO SEE if I could talk him into coming with me. You could wait a lifetime for my father to take an honest-to-goodness vacation; my mother had, in fact, done just that. By the time he got around to retiring from his post as a bureaucrat for the Department of Energy, she, unfortunately, had passed on to life's ultimate vacation. But if you called Dad and told him you had a job for him to do, the more menial and tedious the better, he would be there in a heartbeat. At various trying times during my adult life, I had asked for his help moving furniture, building shelves, painting the house. These were all acceptable ways of saying how much I really needed my dad—without the emotional messiness of really admitting it, either to him or to myself.

"Pop, listen, I hate to bother you, but I need your help. I have to go pick up this car down in Dallas and drive it back to New York. Any chance I could get you to join me for three long days of driving, bad food, and cheap motels?"

"Sounds great! When do we start?"

Chapter Two

OUT OF EGYPT

THE BIG DAY.

Rose and the boys and I squeezed into Speedy and headed upstate. Spike rode with us going from lap to lap, deciding whom to puke on when she got carsick.

We drove across the George Washington Bridge, up the Palisades Parkway to the New York State Thruway, took the Kingston exit for the long haul up into the Catskills on Route 28 through the hamlets of Hurley, West Hurley, Phoenicia, Ashokan, Fleischmanns, Arkville, Margaretville, and, finally, to Delhi.

There is something familiar about these towns, even the first time you see them. Your windshield frames the Catskills as a life-size "Wish You Were Here" postcard. Margaretville was where Rose and I had bought that old farmhouse back in the old, fun, careless days before marriage, mortgages, kids, and all the rest. Rose's parents, Ruth and Saul, had a place a couple of towns over, in Delhi. Rose and the boys would spend the next five days there while I picked up "the Blue Beckham Bomber" in Dallas, a new air conditioning system was installed in our apartment in New York, and, we hoped, somewhere "up there," God, the Fates, Vishnu, whatever party responsible, decided it was time for our family's luck to change.

While Delhi was our official destination, driving upstate was synonymous for me with Bailey Farm, a trip down memory lane to that place where, once upon a time, Rose and I had been happy.

Our lives together began with a kiss good-bye.

Before that kiss we were just two colleagues at an office party. I went in for what I thought would be just a friendly "peck" goodnight, but the moment our lips touched, something altogether different, on a whole other order of magnitude, occurred.

"Wow," I said after we kissed, feeling wobbly from more than just wine.

"Yeah," Rose agreed, leaning back against the wall for support.

I felt suddenly naked with her, even with our clothes on.

Which was a little awkward considering that we were in a room full of people. I felt every pair of eyes in the room on us—including those of the very nice Jewish doctor that Rose was dating at the time. I took an awkward step back, stumbling over my feet and my words at the same time.

"Well . . . I, ah . . . I should really be, you know—"

Rose looked in my eyes. "You're not leaving," she said. Not a come-on or a command, just a statement of fact that, the moment she said it, seemed like the most beautifully obvious thing in the world. I wasn't going anywhere. Not without her. Ever again. The sensation of falling in love is as close to experiencing a divine presence as most of us will ever know in this life. We are touched and moved by a power bigger than ourselves, "bigger than both of us." We "fall" in love; this greatness is thrust upon us.

Not that Rose and I were fighting it.

Two weeks after that fateful kiss, we decided it was time for me to meet Rose's family. The invitation was for Passover. This, I understood vaguely, was a Jewish thing. I didn't know from Jewish. I had grown up in the lands of the white bread—Iowa, Minnesota, and Virginia. Most of what I thought I knew about Jewish I had cribbed from watching *The Ten Commandments*.

In the movie, Charlton Heston plays Moses, the deliverer, who leads the Israelites out of Egypt to the promised land. Growing up, Moses didn't know that he was Jewish, having been raised, through one of those cruel accidents of fate that abound in old books and movies, in the house of Pharaoh as a prince of Egypt. The Passover happened one night when "I-Am-That-I-Am," the Popeye-ish name God calls himself, gets sick and tired of the Egyptians making his chosen people, the Israelites, eat the bread of affliction and sends an angel of death—which, in the movie, looks suspiciously like dry ice fog—to take the first-born sons of Egypt so that Pharaoh finally gets the point and lets the Jews have their Exodus already.

I always liked that movie. You gotta love real men like Charlton Heston and Yul Brynner who could still look like real men wearing costumes that were really dresses. I loved the highfalutin way that everybody in the movie talks, like when Moses comes upon the shepherd girl, Sephora, tending to her flock on the foothills of "I-Am-That-I-Am's" mountain and the two of them decide to settle down and be Bedouins together.

SEPHORA

Our tents are not the columned halls of Egypt,
but our children play happily before them. We can
offer you little, but we offer all we have.

MOSES

I have not little, Sephora. I have nothing.

SEPHORA

Nothing from some is more than gold from
others.

MOSES

You would fill the emptiness of my heart?

SEPHORA

I could never fill all of it, Moses, but I shall not be
jealous of a memory.

When Rose and I met, I, like Moses, had plenty of emptiness
in my heart and was profoundly grateful to have met a woman
who wanted to help me fill it. I had been wandering in the vast,
navel-gazing desert of my own loneliness since the day I became
a man.

In the Jewish faith, a boy becomes a man at the age of thirteen.
In the modern Bar Mitzvah ceremony, each son of Israel is required
to recite a portion of the Torah during the Saturday Shabbat services, after which there is much dancing and catering to be enjoyed
by all.

In my family, there was no catering when you became a man. No
blessings. The only oaths you swore were of the unprintable variety.

In my family, you became a man when you could lock Mom in
the closet. In this rite, the mother threatens to beat her son with a

stick, and the son proves that he has the physical strength to take the stick from her and then threatens to beat her with it if she doesn't cease and desist.

Mom's strange and profound unhappiness was a dark well—and a mystery—that she never got to the bottom of. Her efforts to make sense of her pain and heal herself turned the last twenty-five years of her life into a traveling medicine show of anything New Age or alternative. Her last guru-of-the-month was the Enlightened Fred, arguably our foremost channeler of Ramada, a beneficent and healing spirit not, to my knowledge, affiliated with the hotel chain.

For me and my two older brothers, Kirk and Paul, taking the stick from my mother's hand was kind of like that scene in the TV show *Kung Fu* in which the monk takes the pebble from the master's hand and then the master intones, "Time for you to leave." My brothers and I did not let the screen door hit us on the way out. Kirk and I left before we graduated from high school, Paul shortly after. For the most part, Kirk and Paul had the good sense to stay gone, but I was the baby of the family and kept coming back, like a lost puppy, looking for scraps from my parents' table.

They gave us what they could. They weren't bad people; we just weren't a very good family. My mother couldn't deal with the world, and my father couldn't deal with my mother, and so he just went to the office and Mom just went nuts. Raising my brothers and I was something that got lost in the shuffle somewhere between "nuts" and "the office." I always felt like I survived my family more than I belonged to it. Maybe that's why my favorite part of *The Ten Commandments* is where Moses finds out that the unjust Egyptians who raised him were not his true family.

If Charlton Heston could pass for Jewish, maybe I could too.

"HOW IS TONIGHT DIFFERENT from all other nights?"
This is the question that kicks off the Passover dinner, a ceremonial meal to commemorate how "I-Am-That-I-Am" smote the first-born sons of those pesky Egyptians, passing over the sons of the God of Abraham, to finally convince Pharaoh to release the Hebrew slaves from their centuries of bondage.

At my first Passover dinner with Rose's family, just three weeks after we started dating, I sat next to Rose, holding her hand underneath the table while her father, Saul, a retired pediatrician, read aloud the traditional answers to the question of why that night was different from all other nights—on Passover, they recline to celebrate their status as free men while eating bitter herbs and unleavened matzo bread to remember how their ancestors were forced to eat the bitter bread of affliction and had to flee Egypt. (I just have to put in here, based on my personal taste test, the bread of affliction must have been unsavory stuff indeed for matzo to be considered an improvement.)

As the meal progressed and the wine and conversation flowed, I came up with my own answers for how this night was different from all others.

First of all, a girlfriend had asked me to meet her family, and I hadn't run for the hills. Throughout my twenties, I'd been commitment averse in the extreme. Especially with the girls I'd really liked. Based on growing up with my parents, marriage was the last thing I'd want to do to someone I loved. Not only did I meet Rose's family that night, but I liked them. I liked the way they liked each other. A family dinner in Rose's house was different from the ones that happened in my house just for being a family dinner that actually happened. After my brothers and I left home, a good year for our family was one in which we all sat down together at the same table even once.

I liked how easily everyone laughed in the house of Rose.

And how easily they complained. Even the men.

"The brisket was a bit dry this time, I'm afraid, Ruth," Saul said to Rose's mother, as I looked on, speechless. I had assumed that, like the bitter herbs and the unleavened bread, there had been a symbolic significance to the brisket, that the dryness of the meat was meant to remind the Jewish people of the aridness of the desert they crossed while fleeing Egypt. But even if the brisket was irreligiously dry, to complain was sacrilege for men of my tight-lipped Midwestern tribe. This made hearing Saul whine about the brisket liberation itself to me. The kvetch of freedom.

And I liked how the conversation never ebbed in the house of Rose.

The God of my father was worshipped only in silence. Our family dinners, when they happened, started with "a moment of silence" that was typically observed for the duration of the meal. Lulls in conversation seemed to last for days, weeks, months. Over our family table hung Ingmar Bergman–size clouds of unspoken despair so massive I'm sure they showed up on Doppler radar. I think it was in these silences at the dinner table that I, quite by accident, became a writer—coming up with jokes, anecdotes, observations, anything to keep at bay that awful silence.

Rose's love was my Exodus, my ticket out of Egypt.

OUR WEDDING TOOK PLACE in our beloved Margaretville on a rainy October morning a little more than a year after that fateful Passover dinner. A Jewish rabbi presided over the service, and all my Midwestern relatives made grand fools of themselves dancing to the traditional klezmer music. Imagine *Fiddler on the Roof* staged in Lake Wobegon.

Rose and I each prepared some words to share as part of the ceremony. Mine took the form of a poem, the first line of which was, "We have nothing in common." Some members of the congregation were heard to gasp at this point in the proceedings.

"Don't worry," I said to all assembled, "it gets better."

The poem in full:

> We have nothing in common
> Except—
> This us
> This everything
> This place
> Closer than hands
> Where at last
> I am home.

It takes a great woman to make a man write bad poetry.

Then it was Rose's turn: "I remember talking to my grandfather Hyman before he died and telling him how great my life was going—work was amazing, I had lots of friends, I couldn't believe that I had saved enough money to buy my first apartment, and Grandpa Hy just looked at me and said, 'Now, if you only had luck.' He meant to find a husband, get married, to finally do all the things that a good Jewish girl should do in life. And then I met Mark and now . . . now, I have luck."

After saying these words to all assembled, she turned to me, her beautiful green eyes wet with joy as she looked deep into mine. I couldn't help touching her. My hand found hers and we clasped for the rest of the ceremony. Nothing is as soft as the touch of a woman who believes in her man.

I was her luck all right.

She just didn't know what kind.

Our first year together was bliss. While the traditional gift for the first anniversary is paper, I had something a little grander in mind. I cut the first word of my poem, "We," out of wood, shaped and sanded the letters by hand, and placed them at the center of a collage of things representing the precious moments of our first year together—a sprig from her wedding bouquet and paint swatches for the farmhouse outside Margaretville that we renovated together.

In the years that followed, I did similar collages around the words "have" and "nothing"—the next two words in the wedding poem. These collages included pictures of our friends on happy weekends up at Bailey Farm and Sam's birth announcement. My grand plan was to continue on that way, illuminating each successive word in the wedding poem with happy memories so that after twenty-one years we would have this huge, sofa-size representation of our love, the promise of that magical first kiss fulfilled.

Unfortunately, I got sidetracked by our year from hell and only got as far as:

We—have—nothing . . .

Those words hung on the wall, an un-funny joke, haunting us.

"HOW WAS YOUR FLIGHT from D.C., Pop?" I said, giving him our traditional greeting, the backslapping, one-armed real man's half-hug, when we finally met in the passenger pick-up area outside the Dallas airport. Dad had moved our family east to the Washington, D.C., area to take a job with the Department of Energy back when I was in high school, and he had recently retired there.

"Just fine," he said with a smile. He's a good-looking man, my dad, in that accidental way that I work hard to emulate: a face craggy and strong, well framed by his white beard. His bushy eyebrows sheltered his watery blue eyes like thatched roofs. He was dressed in his daily uniform since retiring from his post as a senior government official—jeans and a flannel shirt.

My father was best man at my wedding. It was largely a political choice on my part. Selecting Dad allowed me to sidestep the impossible task of tapping just one of my brothers or best friends for the honor. And I could tell it meant a lot to Dad. As we got into our rented tuxedos that morning, dressing quickly but carefully, like firemen, men with a job to do, Dad's always-ruddy face was pink to bursting from the physical effort of holding his feelings in check. Not a healthy color.

"You're not having a heart attack are you, Dad? Because that would suck," I said with my usual tact and tasteful humor.

"No. Just a . . . a big day for me. I . . . ah . . . I was just thinking about . . . ," he said, eyes misty.

Wow, this might be it right here, I thought—*the day I actually see my father cry.*

"Yes, Dad, what were you thinking about?" I said, touched that he would end his decades-long drought on my wedding day, opening up his waterworks in my honor.

"I was thinking about . . . a pine tree I saw this morning."

"A pine tree?"

"I was taking a walk early this morning, and I saw this . . . this old tree that had lived through a forest fire. At first you just saw the scorched trunk and stubs of the branches. The tree looked dead. But if you looked closer, you saw these tiny sprouts of new life coming out of the trunk. It was a . . . a great tree."

Dad then put his hand on my shoulder and nodded significantly at me, as if glad we had had this little talk, and then went back to futzing with his cummerbund.

Once you get to know my father, it's actually not so surprising that he would identify so closely with a piece of wood. My father's emotions seem as foreign a language to him as Yiddish is to me. Just as, if I ever attempted to say, "Rose, I love to eat your mother's Jewish cooking because it's delicious," it might as easily come out as "Rose, I love to eat your delicious mother because she's Jewish," the feelings my father had meant to express with his story about the pine tree were lost in translation.

It wasn't his fault; while the Inuit people may have thirty-seven different words for snow, the men of my father's generation have only one catchall word to cover all emotions: "Fine."

"How about your flight?" Dad asked.

"Oh, fine."

"Good. How are my grandkids doing?"

"Great."

"And Rose?"

"Oh, you know . . . fine, I guess."

Dad nodded slowly, understanding everything or nothing, I wasn't sure.

"Hey, it's warm down here," he finally said.

"Sure is."

"Well, I guess Texas really is the South so . . . that figures."

"Yep . . ."

And, with that, we had completely exhausted our family's entire supply of small talk. Rose once leaned over to me during the ceremonial "moment of silence" my family observes before dinner and whispered, "How about a moment of conversation?" Dad and I just stood there in ARRIVALS blinking at each other in the Texas sunshine, waiting for Bill, my eBay seller, to pick us up.

Fifteen hundred miles, three days, two men, one car, and zero small talk—any route we took was going to be the long way home.

After a mercifully short interval, Bill, the salesman/deacon from whom I had bought the Blue Beckham Bomber on eBay, pulled up in a grand steamboat of a Lexus, a like-new alabaster 430, and Dad and I climbed aboard. Bill in-person exactly fit the voice I had heard on the phone. Sandy hair flecked with gray, eyes that crinkled behind his gold glasses when he smiled his "aw, shucks" grin. There was something deeply appropriate about him in a business-casual sort of way, as if there had been no moment in his adult life, with the possible exception of his wedding, that had not called for the blue button-down shirt and freshly pressed chinos he now wore.

We drove past the confines of the airport, through the sprawling outskirts of the Dallas–Fort Worth Metroplex—a big nowhere of places waiting to become places, all of it "prime" real estate, at least if you believed the developers' signs.

"Thanks for picking us up," I said to Bill.

"No trouble at all."

"Sorry to make you work on a Sunday," Dad chimed in.

"Well, there's always a little something going on, keeps things interesting. Ain't this a honey of a day?"

I love the way Texans talk, so unlike us tight-lipped Midwesterners. They can make conversation out of thin air, about nothing at all. It's conversation in its purest form, really: a warm background of syllables, a nice little area rug of consonance to furnish the common space you're sharing with an acquaintance who just became your new best friend. We rode a long welcome mat of conversation all the way to Bill's BMW dealership, where the Blue Beckham Bomber waited to change my life, I hoped for the better.

THE BLUE BECKHAM BOMBER glistened in the sun like the paint was still wet. Mint as new money. Bill handed me the keys. I got in. The door closed with a deeply satisfying bank vault "WHUMP." The leather seats were the color of honey and soft as a baby's butt. Burled walnut and inlaid boxwood wrapped around the cabin like a nice, big, they-just-don't-make-'em-like-this-anymore hug. I turned the key. The throaty V8 rumbled pleasantly to life like a sleepy giant humming a little Bavarian ditty about tearing down the Autobahn to grandmother's house at a hundred and fifty miles an hour.

Bill got in the backseat and Dad rode shotgun as we took the Bomber for a test drive. I wanted to feel . . . what? Something magical. Something on the order of the trumpet trills that greeted General Patton when he came to a field of battle that told me *I had been there before*, that this meeting was fated.

What I had instead was Bill's voice in the backseat, telling me to get over into the right lane to exit the freeway so we could loop around and head back.

"What'd you think?" Bill asked as we returned to the dealership's parking lot.

You had me at "CLICK HERE TO BUY IT NOW."

After doing my best to appear knowledgeable and discerning, kicking the tires and grasping at dipsticks, the final papers were exchanged and the car was mine. Dad and I put our bags in the trunk, took pictures with Bill in front of the car like this was an event worthy of a ribbon cutting, and then Dad and I got in the Bomber and drove off—I wish I could say "into the sunset," but it was high noon.

Chapter Three

CLOUD CITY AND THE DELTA

"**W**AGONS HO!**" Dad called out with a fist pump as we hit the open road in the Bomber. "I'm really glad we're getting this father-son time together."

"Me too," I said.

"I've really been looking forward to it," he said with an earnest nod. I don't know why, but when he's working this hard to say exactly the right thing, it always rubs me the wrong way. Like he's looking for a free pass for all the years he was too busy working to really talk to me.

"Uh-huh. Look, Dad, you know, I might have a little work to do."

"Work?"

"Just a little bit. I'm sure I mentioned it."

"I don't think so."

"Must have slipped my mind. It's just been so busy."

"It's all right."

"I'm sorry—"

"It's fine."

My father and I had played out versions of this dialogue count-less times, but this was maybe the first time *I* was the one taking our father-son time for granted. I had a magazine story that I had to finish while we were on the road to get it to my editor before deadline.

Dad turned to look out the window of the Bomber, lips pursed. For him this was shouting. It slowly dawned on me that I had hurt his feelings, made him feel like a tag-along. Shit. I felt for the guy.

Karma's a bitch.

When I was growing up, Dad was such a workaholic that one fine Sunday afternoon when I was fourteen, he dispatched his second-in-command to fill in for him—not at work, but to spend quality time with me. At first, I felt honored that Dad saw me as such a high priority that he sent not some low-level underling but his right-hand man, a warm, overstuffed couch of a guy named Ted Kapurakus, to take me to see *The Empire Strikes Back*. But as the movie wore on, and the awkwardness of sharing popcorn with a near stranger in a dark movie theater sunk in, it slowly dawned on me that my dad was full of shit.

Near the end of *The Empire Strikes Back*, the part where Darth Vader tells Luke, "I am your father," I turned to look at Ted Kapurakus—was *he* actually my father? Was that the real reason I was having this father-son time with *him*? I studied his strong Greek profile, the way his comfortable bulk overflowed the movie theater seat next to mine, the dark hair on his thick, meaty knuckles as he dug into our shared bucket of popcorn. I'm a rangy hay-seed from Iowa. Ted Kapurakus and I shared only slightly more DNA than I did with our brothers the apes. And yet, that a man who sent an employee to spend "quality time" with his son could, in good conscience, call himself my father seemed almost equally absurd. I turned back to face the movie screen:

EXT. CLOUD CITY—DAY

> VADER
>
> Luke, join me, and together we can rule the
> galaxy as father and son. Come with me. It is the
> only way.
>
> LUKE
>
> I'll never join you!

Luke steps off the platform into space, with only the clouds below to break his fall.

I WAS WITH LUKE—I, too, would rather throw myself off a bridge than end up like my dad. My approach to parenting basically boiled down to asking myself, WWDD? (*What would Dad do?*) And then doing roughly the opposite. He was an absentee father and so I became Mr. Mom. And this Mr. Mom had a chip on his shoulder, something to prove. It was a notch in my belt that I changed more diapers than Rose. That when things went bump in the night, it was *my* name they called out to make them feel safe. I wasn't just rais-ing my boys, I was "schooling" the memory of my father, showing him how the job was done.

I looked over at Dad riding shotgun next to me as we approached the Texas-Louisiana border. The whir of the air conditioner blowing ice cold seemed deafening, drowning out everything but the silence between us.

"Dad, look," I said finally, "I'll call my editor. See if I can get some more time."

"Oh, you don't have to," he said innocently. He smiled, being big about the whole thing—which irked the crap out of me. If he thought *he* was the one who got to let *me* off the hook for turning family time into work time, I had a lifetime supply of baggage that said otherwise.

"Do you remember that day I got to see you at work?" I asked casually.

"Umm . . . not sure."

Denial will not work with me, old man. The student has become the master.

"It was over spring break my junior year of college. You let me come in to use one of the computers at your office after mine crashed in the middle of that long paper?" (It was a twenty-page term paper on *Nausea* by Jean-Paul Sartre that I cheekily entitled "*Nausea* Ad Nauseam." Ah, youth . . .)

"Oh, yeah . . . that was something," Dad finally said with a smile that looked more like a wince. This was the one and only take-your-kid-to-work day I was ever granted.

What my father did all day had been the great mystery of my youth.

I thought, perhaps, he was a spy. He would leave for work early each morning, often before dawn, and, twelve to fourteen hours later, return home. What happened in those intervening hours was a subject rarely, if ever, discussed in our home.

What was this mysterious place he disappeared to every day, *the office*?

In search of an answer, I would pick through what scraps of my dad were left at the end of the day, sifting through the tiny pieces of him that had accumulated on top of his dresser: the piles of change, the dried-out pens, the neat stacks of business cards like dance cards for people waiting to claim his time, and the great wealth of paper clips—my father, it seemed, was a man who always needed something on hand to help him keep it all together.

I would open my father's closet and wonder at the vivid sport coats (this was the '70s) and the off-the-rack armada of polyester ties, edges sharp as swords, waiting to be deployed at my mother's command because, as she repeatedly complained, my father could not be trusted to dress himself. Left to his own devices, he was liable to take Robert F. Kennedy's words about men of vision seeing what wasn't there and asking "Why not?" and apply it to the pairing of plaid with paisley, or checks with stripes. My mother told him repeatedly that these combinations simply would not "do," but Dad didn't listen.

Now, when you're a kid, dressing yourself and being a good listener are pretty much your métier, so Dad's failure to develop these core competencies disturbed me. Every boy sees his father as special; but as I grew up, I was forced to consider the possibility that my dad might be the kind of "special" that gets you a place in the Olympics that no one watches on TV. The only time I really saw Dad was at the end of a long workday when he was so exhausted that simple questions like "Can we play catch?" or "When can you help me with my book report?" led him to dumbly stammer, "Ah . . . let's see, I . . . um . . . " By the time I got into my teens, it seemed impossible to me that this numbnut could hold down *any* job, let alone be a senior government official.

And so, when my one and only take-your-kid-to-work day finally arrived, seeing my dad in action at the Department of Energy was nothing short of a revelation.

Imagine you're Clark Kent's son and you never knew Daddy was Superman.

The bumbling, stuttering shell of a man I knew at home transformed himself before my eyes into a dynamic, authoritative presence. Every time he stepped out of his corner office, he was like an NBA point guard coming off the bench, running a fast break to the coffee machine as subordinates came flying at him with papers that needed signing, expenditures that needed authorizing, hands that needed holding.

"Mr. Millhone, are you sure you want *me* to go to the Paris conference this year?" said Bob, a slump-shouldered senior analyst who clearly looked up to my dad as the father figure I never knew I had.

Dad's play was a thing of beauty. ESPN *SportsCenter* highlight-reel worthy. Without breaking stride on his fast break to the coffee machine, he turned and dished Bob a clutch affirmation: "Absolutely, Bob—why should I be the one to go to Paris when you've done all the research? You'll do a better job than I will. I want you there." Dad gave him a pat on the back, and old Bob beamed like an earnest schoolboy who just got a gold star on his forehead.

The great ones always make it look easy.

I watched all this from the cheap seats, a secretarial station I had commandeered to work on my Sartre paper, with my jaw dropped somewhere in the vicinity of my shoes. Did I just see that? Who was that masked man?

"Your father," Bob said, standing at the urinal next to mine later that day, "is the greatest boss I ever had. He's just a great man, period. But you're his son—you know that already."

After Bob finished his business at the urinal and strode off humming "La Marseillaise," headed for Paris, I thought to myself:

Actually, Bob, I had no idea.

How come Bob, this stranger, knew my father better than I did? Why did his co-workers get his best, get to feast on all he was, while my brothers and I had to fight over whatever scraps were left of him at the end of the day? While this isn't the whole answer, I think the men of my father's generation got sold a bill of goods that being a man consisted entirely of going to work. It wasn't the best deal for their families, but it was no bargain for them either.

On the subway ride home that evening, I watched my father's shoulders stoop, the twinkle in his eyes dim, as if every stop closer to our house was another dose of kryptonite. Just before we were about to get off the subway, he spoke to me, in the halting, exhausted stammer I knew as the voice of my father:

"I'm, ah . . . really glad you, um . . . had the chance to see me at work. I . . . um . . . often think that I . . . I do a better job as a . . . a boss and an administrator . . . than I do, ah . . . as a husband and a father."

This was the really annoying thing about my dad: He's a profoundly decent and painfully honest man, aware of his shortcomings and big enough to admit them. If the guy was going to be an absentee father, the least he could do was let me hate him for it.

DAD AND I GOT OFF THE ROAD sometime after night-fall, somewhere near Baton Rouge, Louisiana. After starting the day in New York, before sunrise, I was too tired to know or care. I parked the Bomber outside our motel room, keying on the car alarm and patting the warm hood to tuck it in for the night.

Our motel room was remarkable only for its sameness to every other chain motel room I'd ever been in—the same beige walls, the same plastic cups sanitation-sealed for my safety and convenience, the same synthetic yet homey bedspread. As Dad and I got into our beds and grunted good night, I drowsily wondered if we would also have the same dreams as all the other people who had stayed in this room.

Just as this thought was giving way to the next little breadcrumb of nonsense on the path to sleep, my cell phone rang. I clicked on the light, fumbled to answer it.

"Hello?" I said in a voice I hoped sufficiently sleepy to nip any chitchat in the bud.

"We have a crisis," Rose said.

I was instantly wide-awake.

"What's going on?"

"It's Sam—"

The phone cut out for a moment as the call waiting interrupted with an incoming call on her end.

"What's the matter with Sam?"

"Hold on."

I held on . . . and on . . . long enough to imagine any number of horrible accidents that could have befallen Sam and led to this dreaded phone call in the middle of the night. Maybe a car accident at that blind corner where the winding country road up to Saul and

Ruth's place meets up with Route 28? Or maybe Sam fell down the stairs onto those hard terrazzo tiles in their entryway. I warned him not to play there! My face felt hot. The plastic cell phone became slippery in my sweaty palm. *Calm down*, I told myself. *Use your head. Be logical.* Right. Still holding on for Rose, I got out of bed and started packing my bag. Always be prepared. How far were we from an airport? Could I get a flight to upstate New York? Cooperstown must have an airport. That was the nearest level-four trauma center to Delhi, and knowing Rose, she'd insist they take Sam there if it was anything really serious. Would the medevac helicopter have enough space to land on the lawn next to Saul and Ruth's house?

"What's wrong?" Dad said, rolling over.

"It's Sam," I said calmly, handling it well. My hands weren't even shaking.

"Is he okay?" Dad asked.

"I'm holding on for Rose to give me the details," I said, putting the phone down to pull a T-shirt over my head. I already had my jeans on.

"Hello? *Hello?!*" Rose was saying on my cell phone as I picked it back up.

"I'm here."

"I can't deal with this!" she said.

"Okay honey, just calm down. Tell me what happened."

"I'm dealing with barbarians!"

"*Barbarians?*" There was no page in *The Worst-Case Scenario Survival Handbook* regarding barbarians.

"Yes! I'm getting no favored nations, no concessions, nothing. This negotiation is going to go all night!"

"I meant with *Sam*. You said there was a crisis."

"Right. I'm sorry, it's just been—"

"What's the crisis?!"

"Well, Sam doesn't want to go to bed."

"*That's* your fucking crisis?! That's what all this is about?!"

"All *what* is about? Why are you yelling at me?"

I sighed, wiping the cold sweat from my brow as I flopped down on my bed.

"Sam's okay?" Dad asked. I nodded.

"Start over," I said to Rose with a sigh.

"Sam had one of his bad dreams again. I tried to comfort him but he wanted you."

"Okay."

"What do you mean, okay?"

"I mean . . . okay, I understand."

"No, you don't. He wanted *you* to comfort him and you weren't even here."

"You want me to talk to him?"

"Fine."

She slammed the phone down, and after a moment, Sam picked up.

"Dad, I really, really miss you."

"I miss you too, Sporto. Having fun at Grandma and Grandpa's?"

"Kind of. It's more funner when you're here."

"I know. But Mommy's there."

"She's had to work a lot."

"That happens."

"I don't like it."

"I don't think Mommy likes it either."

"Yeah . . . she's using a lot of not-nice words."

"Well, not-nice words, ah . . . happen. Isn't it past your bedtime, Sporto?"

Radio silence.

"You have another bad dream?"

"Yeah."

"You want to talk about it?"

"No."

"No, huh? That's too bad," I said, getting up to pace. I think better when I'm moving. "So you called me up to *not* talk to me, goof-a-saurus?" I said, playing for time as Dad watched me pace from his bed.

"You know what?" I finally said. "I think bad dreams are actually a good thing."

"Dad, that makes no sense."

"Bad dreams teach you what you're afraid of."

"But Dad, I already know what I'm afraid of."

"Okay, smarty-pants. What are you afraid of?"

"Snakes."

"What kind of snakes?"

"Cobras—like we saw on the nature channel."

"Is that what you dreamed about tonight?"

"Yeah. They were biting me."

"Huh," I said thoughtfully, giving my complete and undivided attention to *not* thinking about the psychological implications of Sam continuing to have nightmares about various animals biting him more than a year after being bitten by our family dog.

"You know what I think?" I said finally. "I think you're very smart. It's very smart to be afraid of cobras. If you see a cobra on the street, you should definitely run the other way."

"Dad, that's silly—cobras are only in, like, Africa and India. There are no cobras in New York except at the zoo."

"Are you in the zoo?"

"No, I'm at Grandma and Grandpa's house."

"No cobras?"

"Of course not."

"Great, then you don't have to be afraid of cobras anymore and you can go back to bed."

"Da-a-ad," he said, giving it three syllables. "You tricked me."

"A little bit. But I still think you're very smart. And very brave."

"I love you, Dad."

"I love you, too, Sporto." I heard him yawn. "What do you say, pal, bedtime?"

Sam deliberated. "Can I get Chips Ahoy! for bed-night snack?"

"It's a deal. Have your people call my people."

"What?"

"Just put Mommy on the phone. Sleep well, buddy."

"Good night, Dad."

Rose picked up the phone.

"I got him to agree to bedtime, but it's going to cost you—Chips Ahoy! for bedtime snack. That's nonnegotiable."

"That's it? You pick up the phone and presto, everything's milk and cookies?"

"What's wrong?"

"He just wanted you and you're not even here."

"Well, he got me, okay? I talked to him," I said defensively.

"Mr. Fix-It."

"Isn't that who you wanted me to be?"

"No, damn it!"

"So . . . you weren't calling me for help, you just wanted to give me a guilt trip for not being there?"

"Just FYI—I'm really not the bitch you think I am."

I looked up and saw that Dad was watching me. I retreated to the bathroom to try to let him sleep.

"Would you at least tell me what we're arguing about?" I said after closing the bathroom door.

Suddenly Rose was crying. She is simultaneously the most formidable and the most fragile person I have ever known. It knocks me out.

"Sam should be able to talk to *me*," she finally said.

"Honey, you were working," I said, trying to make her feel better.

"I am *tired* of busting my ass just so you get to be super-daddy all the time."

Whether she'd been aiming to or not, this punched my buttons. I came out swinging: "Well, if you spent more time with the boys, I wouldn't have to be Mr. Mom."

"Well, if you made more money, maybe I'd finally get a chance to be a mother to my children."

"You really have a gift for emasculation, you know that?"

Her call waiting clicked in again. Identity crisis on line one.

"God damn it—" she said, clicking off.

I sat for a moment, trying to cool off as I stared at the cold white tiles of the motel bathroom. I pulled the plastic wrap off one of the glasses that had been sanitized for my convenience and drank some water. If only my marriage could be sanitized for my convenience. Marriages are like tofu, they take on the flavor of everything else around them. Our marriage never seemed to lose the aftertaste of our year from hell.

"Everything okay?" Dad asked when I came out of the bathroom.

"Everything is, ah . . . fine," I said, plugging in my cell phone to charge. "Sorry to wake you."

"No, it was a . . . a pleasure watching you work," Dad said, yawning. "You're a good father to those boys."

"Ah . . . thanks," I said, a little surprised to get his vote of confidence after I'd spent all of my angry-young-man years telling him all the things he'd done wrong. I took off my clothes and got back into bed, then stared up at the textured ceiling that all cheap motel rooms seem to have and missed the feeling of missing my wife. I used to miss her. Even one night away seemed an eternity. Now it was a relief.

"Dad?"

"Uh-huh," he said sleepily.

"Can I ask you something?"

"Uh-huh . . . "

"You and Mom had your . . . disagreements." (It is hard to overstate how much of an understatement this is. Saying that my parents had their disagreements is like calling the Civil War a misunderstanding between friends.)

"Uh-huh . . . "

"How the hell did you make it through fifty years together?" My parents celebrated their golden wedding anniversary shortly before my mother died last year.

Dad paused, coughed to clear his throat and then . . .

He snored.

I chuckled. This was actually about as eloquent an answer as I could have hoped to get. Dad knew how to turn off, tune out. Mom used to complain that even when Dad was in the same room, he could be a million miles away.

I pulled out my laptop to try to finish up the magazine story I owed my editor so that I wouldn't have to worry about it for the rest of the trip. We were now near Baton Rouge. Dad and I planned to head east across the Mississippi Delta to New Orleans and then turn north. The ancient Greeks coined the word *delta*. They noticed that when a river reaches its terminus, the channel often splits, forming a triangular island of sediment. The Greek letter "delta" is shaped like a triangle, hence the coinage. Over time, as the river continues to deposit its load of sediment, these deltas grow ever larger, changing the course of the river. It's amazing how all those little bits of sand and dirt can add up to something that could split the mighty Mississippi.

I never thought anything could split Rose and me. But all the things that had happened to us during our year from hell had settled in a way that had left a vast delta between us.

Chapter Four

KATRINAVILLE

"**HAVE YOU SEEN** the devastation yet?"

This was the question that the motel clerk asked when we checked out of our motel room the next morning and Dad mentioned that we were headed toward New Orleans, or "Katrinaville," as I hear some locals have taken to calling it since the hurricane. The clerk asked the question cheerfully, service-with-a-smile, as blithely as one might say, "Have you seen the Grand Canyon yet?" As if "the devastation" was some kind of tourist attraction.

Which, of course, it *is*.

Since the invention of the T-shirt, the horror that has gone un-commemorated by a souvenir T-shirt has yet to be invented. My favorite for Katrina was one that spoofed the "Got Milk?" ads: "Got FEMA?" Perhaps I was being too hard on the perky hotel clerk. Katrina was old news now. The story had already cast its rainbow across *USA Today*, starting on the front page of the blue News section when the storm first hit, through the green of Money as the financial implications were assessed in its aftermath, then the story got off the bench in the red Sports section for the first game the New Orleans Saints played back in the Superdome, and now Katrina was nearly forgotten, at least as far as *USA Today* was concerned, a tear-jerking blip in the purple of Life.

Seen from the freeway as we sped by in the Bomber, New Orleans actually looked well on its way to rebuilding itself. Scaffolds were everywhere—the entire French Quarter was corseted with them like a woman of a certain age not ready to admit she's lost her figure. But once we got out of New Orleans proper and into the low-lying areas flooded by Lake Pontchartrain, we could see, even from the freeway, that "the devastation" was alive and well and living in Jefferson Parrish. Thousands of acres, thousands of lives—all of it looking like a sandcastle after the tide came in.

The sight was enough to put the fear of God in you, even if you didn't believe in God. Just the awesome power and utter indifference of the storm. You may know the storm's name, but it doesn't know yours. It could take your house and spare your neighbor's—or vice versa. It didn't matter. Not to the storm. The storm just *was*.

I thumbed the temperature wheel on the Bomber's air conditioning control, dialing back the chill, appreciating the tactile fact of how the ridges on the knob met my thumb. When and why had the whole world gone digital? I hated LEDs, the way they burned into your eyes. The Bomber was old enough that it still felt like a car instead of some home computer on wheels—part of why I liked it. It was a good car. Solid and powerful. I felt safe in it the way I remembered feeling safe in the big Chevy Impala station wagon we had when I was a kid.

Dad called it "the Green Machine"—but this was back in the olden days when green was just a color. I loved the clear plastic seat covers with the geometric bumps that Mom had put on to "save the upholstery." From what, she never said. The wide speedometer on the dash made the Green Machine seem infinitely powerful. I spent an entire road trip puzzling out what the "R, D, N, 1, 2" in the small window on the steering column meant. My older brothers, Paul and Kirk, would ride in back while I sat up front, in the middle of the wide bench seat between Mom and Dad. This was back before air bags, back before buckling up was the law, back before everything gave you cancer and a mother could use the push-button cigarette lighter in the center of the dash without shame, the way my mother did for her long, graceful Eve 120s.

"Let me know if you get warm," I said to Dad, who was riding shotgun.

How strange it was to trade places with my father. I remembered one particular night when I was riding shotgun for him in the Green Machine. The lights of the car behind us reflected in our rearview mirror, making Dad look like a bandit in reverse. A storm was coming. A big one. Headed our way. The lightning strobed, giving us moments of daytime, and then came the thunder, a big hammer thudding far away.

"Will the storm hit us? Will it, Dad?" I asked, my little hands sweaty in the dark as I tried to grip the slick plastic seat cover.

Dad looked not at the storm but at me—as if through some scoutmaster trick an old Indian had taught him, he could see in my eyes the path the storm would take.

"Nah . . . it'll go around us," he finally said, nodding slightly, as if letting me in on a secret.

He looked back at the road. The storm was headed directly toward us, like we were driving down the barrel of a gun. But that wasn't what I needed to hear.

Being a father boils down to knowing what lies to tell.

I curled up in his lap and fell asleep while looking up at his eyes, banded with light, staring straight ahead as if trying to keep our car on the road through sheer force of will.

I was doing the same thing now on the Lake Pontchartrain Causeway Bridge—at close to 24 miles long, the longest bridge in the world. Two parallel ribbons of asphalt stretched out into the void. You had to take it on faith that the bridge led somewhere, that there would be another side.

"It looks like we're going to drive off the edge of the world," I said after the monotony of the bridge started getting to me. Nothing to do but just sit there, stare at the road, check the numbers on the odometer to see how much farther it was supposed to be to the other side—if it even existed—and, oh yeah, try to remember not to veer off the bridge and plunge to your death. White-knuckle death by boredom.

The whole thing reminded me way too much of the days and nights I spent staring at the numbers on Benny's vital signs monitor. His status changed hour by hour. For one four-day stretch, I didn't sleep. In Intensive Care, clocks mean nothing. You understand, vaguely, that somewhere out there days are continuing to follow nights the way they used to, but not for you. Time stopped for our family when Benny went into the Neonatal Intensive Care Unit. I stared for hours, and then days, without blinking, almost without breathing, at the numbers on Benny's vital signs monitor to see whether his time was up.

That's what time it is.

Benny was born with amniotic fluid in his lungs. It's a fairly routine thing. It's why the doctor spanks a newborn baby to get him to cry; the baby needs that one good breath that clears out the lungs and fills them with air.

Unfortunately, Benny never got that one good breath.

The fluid in his lungs led to him getting severe pneumonia. His condition deteriorated so rapidly it seemed to be in free fall: Five days after he was born, both of his lungs had collapsed. The doctors gave him antibiotics for the pneumonia and performed emergency surgery to implant a tube in his chest to help reinflate his lungs.

But Benny was still dying.

And they didn't know why.

"Honey, you should go home, get some rest," I said to Rose. I was worried about her. She had gone directly from giving birth to camping out on a couch with me in the parents' room just off the Intensive Care Unit.

Rose shook her head. "I'm not leaving this hospital until he's off the respirator."

"Honey, that could take days, weeks, we don't know at this point."

"I don't care if it takes forever. I'm not leaving him," she declared, the roar of a mama lion.

"Okay," I said, reaching for her hand.

"I just wish I could hold him," she said, as fragile this moment as she'd been fierce the last. Benny had so many tubes and wires plugged into him that he looked like the back of your VCR. This cold embrace was what welcomed him to the world. He couldn't be picked up until he came off the respirator. The breathing tube forced open his mouth like a silent scream. You don't hear babies cry in the NICU. Most of them are too sick. What you hear is the *beep—beep—beep* of all the machines. It sounds disturbingly like a McDonald's. But instead of telling you that the fries are done, these machines beep when an IV has run out, or when a baby has stopped breathing.

Rose and I stayed. We slept—when we could sleep—in shifts so that one of us was at Benny's side at all times. We kept this vigil hour after hour, day after day, test after test—each one requiring Benny to be stuck with a needle. The scale of this needle in relation to his tiny arm seemed roughly approximate to driving a tent pole into mine.

"Do they *have* to do that?" I asked Benny's doctor, Dr. Karen Hendricks-Munoz, as we watched a nurse struggling to find a vein to tap. Eventually the ones in Benny's arms wore out and they had to start piercing his scalp.

"Sorry. We need to measure his oxygen levels," Dr. Hendricks-Munoz said. Dr. H-M, as everyone calls her, is the Chief of Neonatology for both NYU Medical Center and Bellevue Hospital Center. She is a tall, attractive woman who smiles easily even when her eyes betray that she's had less sleep than you can possibly imagine. She's the nicest person you never want to meet, because if you get to know her, chances are it's because your baby is very, very sick.

"I thought the vital signs monitor told you about the oxygen levels," I said.

"That gives us the blood oxygen saturation level, but we need the blood tests to know the P-sat level—how much of the available oxygen is really being metabolized by his tissues. See, blood is essentially the body's delivery system—"

"Like Fed Ex?"

"Sure. The sat level on the monitor tells us how much oxygen is available for delivery in the bloodstream, and the P-sat level here on this lab report tells how much oxygen actually gets where it's supposed to go in the tissues of the body."

"So, the sat level on the monitor is how full the Fed Ex trucks are, and the P-sat level on that slip from the lab is how many signatures they got for on-time delivery?"

"Congratulations, you just passed Hematology 101," Dr. H-M said.

I smiled as I pictured fleets of bright, shiny Fed Ex trucks racing to bring Benny oxygen. *When it absolutely, positively has to get there overnight.*

"May I?" I said, gesturing to the lab slip, about the size of an ATM receipt.

Dr. H-M smiled, handed it to me. We were colleagues now.

"Ninety-nine percent—looks like our patient's getting an A, doctor," I said, handing back the slip.

"Actually, the P-sat level is a four-hundred point scale. For a patient on a respirator receiving pure oxygen, a P-sat number of ninety-nine is actually extremely suboptimal, I'm sorry to say." Dr. H-M placed a comforting hand on my shoulder. As she went on about her rounds, I just stood there, shaking my head.

The glass wasn't half full. It wasn't even half empty.

It was extremely suboptimal.

What if Benny didn't make it?

The cold weight of this question settled on me like standing out in the rain. I felt the fear soak me to the bone, leaving me Novocain numb. It was as if the Secret Service had rushed in and whisked the part of me that feels off to a secure location. My fear was now duck hunting somewhere with Dick Cheney. But so too were my joy, my sorrow, my humor—most of the things that made me a person, at least the person that my wife fell in love with. My vigilance was left behind to hold the fort until the all-clear sounded. He could be a jerk, but he was good in a fight; coolly assessing risk, taking action, never letting emotions get in the way—mine or anyone else's.

The most common complaint you hear about going to the hospital is how long it takes to see a doctor, but I can tell you from experience, you do *not* want to be the one they feel requires their complete and undivided attention.

There came a morning when Benny had more white coats around his crib than there are waiters at a Chinese restaurant. Now this was service. Department chiefs, no less—Pediatrics, Pediatric Cardiology, Pediatric Neurology, Neonatology—all putting their heads together to come up with . . . a hunch.

We like to think of medicine as being as uniformly efficacious as a white lab coat. But medicine, a life science, is sometimes a lot more like *life* than *science*. There's guesswork, gut-calls, prayer. Real men and women wear those white coats, and the difference between doctors who are merely good and those who are truly gifted can be the difference between knowing which notes to play and being a concert pianist.

Or between life and death.

Dr. H-M's hunch was that Benny was suffering from a condition called Persistent Pulmonary Hypertension in Newborns (PPHN), a rare condition for which even just a few years ago, there was no name, let alone cure. All her tests had been to try to confirm this, but all of them had been inconclusive.

PPHN develops when babies have fluid in their lungs at birth. When the baby is in the womb, the major arteries that branch off from the heart are significantly constricted. This performs a very important function in utero. It allows the mother's cardiovascular system to regulate blood circulation for the baby, helping to ensure that his developing heart is not overwhelmed. The reason that they want a baby to cry as soon as he comes out of the womb is because the shock of that one good breath is what tells the baby's body that he is alive in this world. It's time for him to breathe his own air, pump his own blood. Benny never got that one good breath. Essentially, if Dr. H-M's hunch was correct, Benny was dying because he was lost. His cardiovascular system still thought that he was inside the womb.

With PPHN, the baby's heart and lungs can be perfectly healthy, but because the major arteries leading away from the heart are constricted, oxygenated blood gets shunted back into the heart, where it mixes with unoxygenated blood. Key organs don't get the oxygen they need; toxins build up because they're not being circulated out of the tissues. When the blood's delicate pH balance has been lost, life-giving medications no longer work. The fragile newborn's organs fail one by one until his entire system crashes and the baby dies.

"But you can treat it, can't you?" Rose asked Dr. H-M.

"If it is PPHN, then yes, there is a treatment that works in some cases."

"Not all?" Rose asked.

"Mrs. Millhone, your child is very sick."

Rose's face turned the color of the doctor's coat. "I need to call my dad," she said, walking toward the parents' room. I had not been reassured by Saul's absence. Rose's mother, Ruth, had come down to help care for Sam while Rose and I spent our days and nights at the hospital, but Saul had stayed behind in Delhi. As a retired pediatrician, he was in a position to know exactly how scared we should all be about Benny. I believed he worried that if he came to the hospital, Rose would see it in his face and be undone.

"They have a special machine at Columbia-Presbyterian that can be helpful in cases like Benny's," Dr. H-M said to me after Rose left. "It's called ECMO; the machine breathes for him, gives his lungs a chance to recover." She tried to say this like it was good news.

"You mean a . . . a heart-lung machine?" I asked.

"It's similar. I called Columbia-Pres and it's available."

I had to sit down.

"I'm sorry," she said. "We're giving Benny the maximum life support we can give him at this Intensive Care Unit. I don't want to risk transferring him, but if he doesn't stabilize here soon . . ."

I nodded numbly and she pulled up a chair and we sat together at Benny's bedside. Rose came back from the parents' room and joined us.

"Is his condition life threatening?" Rose asked. While I hadn't kept Rose in the dark, I had tried to stay as positive as possible—she had just given birth and I wanted her to be able to rest.

Dr. H-M, not unkindly, said, "I wouldn't be sitting here if it wasn't." She was the Chief of Neonatology for both NYU and Bellevue. As many as fifty critically ill newborns were under her care at any one time, and out of all of those bedsides, the place she felt her personal attention was most needed was here, with our Benny.

"What are you doing for him?" Rose finally said.

"I'm trying to figure out what kind of guy Benny is," Dr. H-M said.

"What kind of a guy he is?" Rose asked.

"If he's a fighter, I'd like to try treating him for PPHN here. But if we have any doubts about his spirit, then the prudent thing would be to transfer him to Columbia-Pres so he can have ECMO."

"ECMO?" Rose asked.

"It's like a heart-lung machine," I said.

"No way! That is *not* happening to my son," Rose said, getting to her feet and going to Benny to hold his tiny hand. This was the Rose I knew and loved.

Looking at her, Dr. H-M smiled a little and said, "My gut tells me your son is a fighter."

Dr. H-M treated Benny for PPHN. The treatment was fairly simple. Nitrous oxide—laughing gas—gets added to the oxygen mixture. If PPHN was the problem, the laughing gas would ease Benny's pulmonary hypertension enough for him to complete his transition to the land of the breathing.

We all held our breath as we waited for Benny to find his.

Dr. H-M was right about Benny.

After he revived, his first act as a person in this world was to grab the breathing tube that had been shoved down his throat and rip it out. He did the same with the tube that had been surgically implanted in his chest to help reinflate his lungs. He ripped that tube out three times before Dr. H-M and her team finally got the message.

Benny was in the house.

He had no more use for their tubes and wires. He had places to be, a life to live.

Chapter Five

RONALD McDONALD'S HOUSE

"**B**ILLY, YOU MARCH BACK HERE this instant, or you're going to get yourself an *un*-Happy Meal for lunch!"

Dad and I had stopped for lunch at a McDonald's after crossing the Lake Pontchartrain Causeway Bridge, and I took part in the collective head swivel as Billy, a little towheaded kid about Benny's age, instantly turned around and dragged his feet all the way back to his mother, an overstuffed fanny-pack of a person, standing next to me in line. Billy had responded so immediately to her threat of making him eat an *un*-Happy Meal that it made me wonder if such a thing actually existed and, if so, how it was different from a regular Happy Meal. Maybe instead of a toy, the kid gets a lump of coal or a little dead bird.

While most of the headshaking around me seemed aimed at Mrs. Fanny-Pack, I found myself taking her side. I had so been there. One time Benny wandered all the way over to the display of movie tie-ins, aka Happy Meal toys, on the other side of our local McDonald's in New York City, ignoring my calls to come back until I finally yelled, "Benny, *you come back here right now*!" This was Manhattan, so *everybody* comes to McDonald's, and let me tell you, you don't know shame until you've had a Hispanic grandmother, a Nazi skinhead, and a gangbanger all looking down their nose at you at the same time.

Benny had strolled back to where Sam and I were waiting in line. He flashed me his mega-watt smile, a smile that said he knew *exactly* how crazy he was making dear old dad, and wasn't this the funnest game?

"Benny, *never* do that. I could lose you, do you understand? I could lose you!"

"Yeah, Benny. Daddy could lose you!" Sam repeated.

Benny nodded like he was a puppet, his head bouncing on a string—the preverbal equivalent of "*whatever.*"

I liked to think that the reason Benny hadn't learned to talk yet was because he hadn't needed to—he already had the world wrapped around his finger. While Rose wanted to believe that as well, this didn't stop her from having him screened for everything from mental retardation to deafness to autism to dengue fever. He had, at long last, been cleared of all the above and was working with a speech therapist. She theorized that having his mouth immobilized by a respirator during his developmentally crucial first days of life was what had caused his speech delays. I hated going to McDonald's because I couldn't look at those little Plexiglas Ronald

McDonald House donation boxes without thinking, *Benny was really sick like those sick kids . . .*

Beep! Beep! Beep!

The electronic fast-food machines screamed for attention like little robot babies. The workers raced about with such urgency you'd almost think they were manning an emergency room instead of the lunch shift at McDonald's.

"Up! Up! Up!" Benny cried, arms outstretched.

Beep! Beep! Beep! The alert tone on the deep-fat fryer sounded exactly like Ben's vital signs monitor from the Neonatal Intensive Care Unit. I unzipped my jacket. *When did it get so hot in here?*

"Daddy, why do they call it a Happy Meal?" Sam asked.

"Would you want something called an *un-Happy* Meal?"

Sam considered the matter. "Would I still get a toy?"

"Ah . . . sure . . . whatever . . . "

My face felt hot as I looked for our cashier in the sea of colorful uniforms rushing back and forth behind the counter. For a split second, I thought I saw a patch of sea-foam green—doctor's scrubs. In my mind's eye, the heat lamps above the French fry station were now the warming lights that mounted above Ben's crib in the NICU. A ribbon of cold sweat rolled down my spine. I couldn't breathe.

Beep! Beep! Beep!

"Up! Up! Up!"

The Happy Meals finally arrived. I grabbed them. Picked up Benny. Squeezed Sam's hand so hard it made him wince. Home. Now.

As I pushed my way down the crowded sidewalk, Benny asked from his perch atop my shoulders, "Da-da . . . okay? Okay?"

"Daddy's fine."

Yeah, right.

"May I take your order, sir? *Sir?*"

The cashier at the McDonald's where Dad and I had stopped after making it across the Lake Pontchartrain Causeway Bridge was now staring at me. I blinked, trying to clear my head, return to the present. It's not so much that I had bad memories of our year from hell—it's more like they had me.

"You okay?" Dad asked as I got back to our table with our tray of food.

"I'm fine. I just, ah . . . really hate McDonald's," I said handing him his filet-o-fish.

"Well, no reason we have to eat here," Dad said.

"It's fine," I said as my cell phone rang. I pretended to be annoyed, but I was grateful for the distraction.

"Hello?" I said.

"Hello, Mr. Mark? It's Nick."

"Sorry, it's the air conditioning contractor," I said to Dad as I took the call.

"How things going up there?" I asked Nick.

"Not good. Your box is maxed out."

"I thought it was just my credit cards that were maxed out."

"Oh, you're funny, Mr. Mark. That's good. Because in my experience, if you don't got a sense of humor, you might as well be roadkill with the bugs crawling in and out of you, stinking up the turnpike."

"In your experience."

"Yes, sir."

"What's the box?"

"The electrical box. You don't got space for another line to run the compressor. I got a guy, a legit guy, licensed and everything, who could do it for you, but it'll cost."

"How much?"

"Five large."

"*Five large?*"

"Five thousand—he has to put in a whole new box."

Yikes.

"But you'll still be able to finish the whole job in the same amount of time, right?" I asked.

Nick just laughed. "That's funny, Mr. Mark. You're a fucking comedian—excuse the language."

I didn't feel funny. I felt like roadkill. That's what Rose was going to turn me into when she got the news that she would, in all likelihood, be coming home to a construction site. I hung up the phone, shaking my head.

"Everything okay?" Dad asked.

"Define *okay* . . . " I said with a sigh. "I just found out that the central air is going to cost double what I thought, and it's not going to get done before we get back, and that is NOT going to go over well. Rose gets these panic attacks if the apartment's a mess."

"Panic attacks?" Dad said, looking up, concerned.

"Panic attacks, insomnia, she doesn't like to leave our room. She's always stressed out, gets ulcers, migraines. She's a mess."

"How long has she been this way?"

"Ever since our year from hell."

"What's she doing for herself?"

"Buying shoes, mostly," I said. "Retail therapy, she calls it."

"Is she seeing someone?"

"Well, she keeps threatening to leave me, but as far as I know, there isn't another man in the picture. Yet."

"I meant, ah . . . someone professionally. For the panic attacks and everything."

"Oh." This seemed like an opportune moment to shove anything in my mouth besides my foot, so I bit into my quarter-pounder to buy some time before answering. "I've tried to get her to see someone, but whenever I push it, she blows up at me. Says I'm just trying to pawn her off on some doctor like her parents," I finally said, resorting to honesty.

Rose's parents first sent her to a psychologist when she was four years old. Rose's father, Saul, was a well-respected pediatrician, and, in being the best father he knew how to be, Saul relied on what he knew best—medicine. Saul grew concerned that his precocious four-year-old daughter, who could converse with any adult on a range of topics, was having trouble fitting in with kids her own age. Instead of scheduling more playdates, he referred her to a specialist, a very nice man named Dr. Wald. While the efficacy of trying to help your daughter adjust to peers her own age by giving her one more adult to talk to on a weekly basis might be easy to criticize in 20–20 hindsight, it was her parents' way of trying to give her the best of everything.

While Rose found her time with Dr. Wald merely confusing, a second round of parent-prescribed psychotherapy when she was fourteen—occasioned by Rose's pilfering a bottle of gin from the liquor cabinet so she could fit in and BYOB at a senior's party—had much more long-lasting side effects. Rose spent her weekly sessions with Dr. Sakinsky smoking cigarettes (ah, the good old bad days), ignoring Dr. Sakinsky, perfecting the fine art of pouting, and thoroughly convincing herself that all forms of talk therapy were a crock of shit; and, furthermore, that her parents were crocks of shit for passing her off to strangers whenever she became too intense, too emotional, too intelligent—in short, too "Rose"—for them to handle.

While Rose eventually got her way (she almost always does), closing the door on her parents' efforts to make her see therapists, these experiences had the unfortunate side effect of also closing the door on therapy should Rose ever actually need psychological help. Say, for example, living through a year where one child almost dies and the other is mauled by a dog right before your very eyes and your marriage starts to fall apart. Little things like that.

"How you doing, guy?" Dad said.

"I'm fine," I said. *Except for the odd panic attack at McDonald's.* I was the calm center of the storm. A rock. Rose accused me of practicing avoidance. I told her, look, even if I knew what that was, with my crazy schedule every day—getting the kids to school, work, renovating our home, teaching at the university, volunteering at the hospital, my new exercise regime, getting the kids to bed while Rose returned work calls to the West Coast—when would I have the time?

I was fine.

This had become one of my most cherished beliefs, that it was *Rose* who needed the professional help. Each family member has his or her roles to play, and I had delegated to Rose the job of having our family's nervous breakdown. This allowed me to keep my emotions safely tucked away in their secure location.

"Are you sure you're okay?"

I didn't say anything at first. Dad, by repeating his inquiry regarding the true nature of my inner status quo, had committed a deliberate and provocative act of near emotional intimacy. One does not just haul off and ask a Midwestern or otherwise emotionally repressed male how he's really doing inside. Not unless you want your head taken off. Men should come with a warning label:

WARNING: CONTENTS UNDER PRESSURE! OPEN AT YOUR OWN RISK!

There are strict rules of engagement one should follow with Midwestern or otherwise emotionally repressed males. For your own protection, always practice the triple-redundant, query-based failsafe system detailed below:

QUERY #1: "How are ya?"

Variants: "How's it hanging?" "What up?"

Whatever form it takes, the hallmark of Query #1 is a basic acknowledgment, presenting a generally positive attitude toward the other party's existence on the planet—and nothing more.

QUERY #2: "Are you sure you're okay?"

Variants: "How you holding up?" "Anything I can do?"

Query #2 is a clear acknowledgment of a pre-existing relationship and signals a willingness to convene a mini-meeting on the spot relating to any piece of old business previously addressed within the confines of said relationship or an introduction of new business, but only if the queried party so chooses.

QUERY #3: "Talk to me, man."

Variants: "Tell me what's really going on." "Dude, it's me."

The striking thing about Query #3 is that it is not a query at all, but a command. By assuming responsibility for the transfer of potentially volatile personal emotional material, the questioner creates a "safe space" in which the questionee can truly let his guard down. The Query #3 protocol must never be attempted before working sequentially through Queries 1 and 2. The questioner should be a trusted friend of long standing or a family member with whom you're currently on good terms. *Mano a mano* exercises of this nature are also best practiced in a safe, secure environment such as a bar, a sporting event, or as an adjunct to physical labor.

The speed with which Dad had escalated our engagement to the Query #2 "Are you sure you're okay?" alarmed me. For *Dad* to notice something was wrong, I must be worse off than I thought. He kept his eyes trained on me as he bit into his filet-o-fish, waiting for me to answer his question.

I opted for a lateral move into blarney: "The thing about having some, you know, really, really, *really* bad days, is that every other day looks pretty great by comparison."

"What do you mean?" Dad asked, not giving an inch. I didn't like being backed into a corner.

"Well, Dad, it's like this," I said, putting more heat on my reply than intended, "after you've seen your son almost die, what else really counts as serious? So what if your marriage is falling apart, I mean, *you'll live*, right?"

"Ah . . . I guess so," Dad said, looking concerned.

I sighed. "That example was just, um, you know, *hypothetical* . . ."

Dad looked at me for a long moment and then nodded. "Sure," he said.

It's the truths we try to cover up that end up being the most naked.

"So, how are *you* doing?" I asked Dad, finally turning the tables on him.

"Oh, you know, fine."

I did know. My father's version of "fine" was struggling to make sense of the world after suffering what I sensitively refer to as his Senior Citizen's Trifecta—retirement, prostate cancer, and the death of his spouse of fifty years—all in the span of six months. That was what my father meant by "fine."

It had taken my entire life, but finally my father and I were starting to speak each other's language.

Chapter Six

BAILEY FARM

YOU'VE GOT TO THINK how they think. Move how they move.

I went on recon, crawling on my hands and knees in our kitchen to inspect all the baby-proofing that I had put in place in anticipation of Benny coming home from the hospital. Cabinet locks—check. Drawer catches—check. Outlet covers—check. I could hear baby Benny burbling and cooing from our bedroom. Since he came home from the hospital a week ago, Rose hadn't let him out of her sight. Even brought him to bed with her—but not to sleep. She worried she might roll over in the night and crush him. She worried that every little rash might be scarlet fever; that every cough was tuberculosis; that the boogeyman was real and out to get us. Things can and do go bump in the night. In the sleepless dark, our fears are more real to us than anything under the sun. When we brought Benny home from the hospital, it wasn't to home-sweet-home but to that place where, statistics show, most accidents occur.

What kind of parents were we?

I completed my recon of the kitchen. Perimeter secure. It would be months before Benny was a crawl threat, but still—never too early to think about safety. I got up off the floor and washed my hands at the kitchen sink. Nine out of ten colds could be prevented if people just washed their hands more regularly. As I dried my hands, I noticed the dog bowls in the dish dryer and put them on the floor. Our dogs, Bailey and Boomer, had been away at a boarding kennel upstate since before Benny was born, and it was time to go pick them up. I put the bowls down on the floor next to the kitchen garbage can and started to walk away and then looked back at my baby-proofed kitchen. Something was wrong.

I hadn't baby-proofed the dogs.

I didn't think either one of them would deliberately hurt the kids, but Bailey was starting to get crotchety in her old age; she had started picking fights with our other dog, Boomer. She would keep trying to eat his food, and suddenly there would be an outburst of blood-curdling growls accompanied by the clash of claws and teeth. While their scrapes never lasted more than a second or two, all the worst stories about kids start with "I just turned my head for a second or two." I had seen a front-page story in the New York *Daily News* about a little girl who ended up getting mauled when she got in the middle of a fight between her family's two dogs, and I couldn't get it out of my head.

"You want to get rid of Bailey?" Rose whispered so that Sam wouldn't hear.

"Of course I don't *want* to—but if it needs to be done, we should do it now. Sam hasn't seen her since before Benny was born. That will make it easier for him to make the transition."

"But we've never *not* had Bailey," Rose said. It was true—we adopted Bailey, a skinny, brindled boxer-pit bull-something mix on the day that Rose and I moved in together.

"Really, how do you feel about this?" she asked.

"I don't," I said. "If I start to feel about it, I won't be able to do what needs to be done."

Rose sighed. "I don't know . . . maybe there's a nice farm somewhere . . . "

I called a friend for advice. Cydney Cross helped us adopt Boomer, the other dog we'd had before Spike. Boomer had brindle markings like Bailey, but if I had to guess as to his breeding, I would say that he was the product of a union between a pit bull and a throw pillow. He was a gentle giant who routinely mistook himself for a Chihuahua, cowering behind me when confronted by a stranger.

I told Cydney about my fears, told her all my heroic efforts, the untold dollars spent on obedience training and doggy Prozac, spun her all my rationalizations for why abandoning Bailey was really the most responsible thing I could do for my family, and braced myself—when Cydney's not rescuing animals in her day job as director of the Mohawk and Hudson River Humane Society in upstate New York, she runs another animal rescue out of her house. She's one of those people.

"I completely understand," Cydney said. "When do you want to put her down?"

"Put her down?!"

"Mark, if I thought Bailey was a dog that people could live with, I would be giving you an earful about how you needed to learn to live with her, but you've tried everything."

"Isn't there some nice farm someplace?"

"Why do people always think there's some farm? There's no farm. I'm sorry, but I'm just not going to be able to place an aging pit bull with an attitude problem."

"That doesn't mean she deserves to die! You can tell people she's okay as long as she's on her medication."

Bailey had been on doggy Prozac for the last three years to help her stop doing things like attacking other dogs on sight and tearing through our apartment chasing an imaginary rabbit like she was having a wide-awake dog dream. The results were mixed. Bailey would stare at the wall, stoned out of her gourd, until the meds wore off and then, hungover I suppose, snap at Boomer until she got her next dose of happy pills.

"An aging pit bull with an attitude problem *and* a drug problem?" Cydney asked. "That doesn't really sweeten the deal. People want puppies. I'm sorry. I know it's hard, but you're doing the right thing."

FOR HER LAST MEAL, I GAVE BAILEY half a box of Purina T-Bonz brand dog treats. It just seemed like the right thing to do. I wanted to make it a good day for her. A good memory. Well, not really a good memory for Bailey. She was going to be, you know, dead. And, on top of that, Cydney told me that dogs don't really have memories. They just sail along in this everlasting now with only their instincts and a few learned behaviors like "sit" and "stay" to guide them. Very Zen.

I decided the way to honor Bailey was to try to make her last day on Earth a dog day. Sail along in that everlasting now. Don't think about the future—there would be plenty of time later to come up with a suitable lie to tell Sam and Ben about what happened to Bailey. And definitely ditch the past. Dwelling upon details like the fact that Bailey had been with us for as long as we had been an "us" would only make it more difficult, if not impossible, to follow through with the big item on our "to do" list for that day:

1) Kill the dog.

I got into the Volkswagen van we had then, the one we got especially for the dogs, to have room to take them with our family wherever we went because they were family too. Even before we added Benny to the brood, if you asked Sam if he had a sister or a brother, he would say yes, he had both—Boomer was his brother and Bailey was his sister.

I was killing his sister.

That was not a helpful thought.

I offered Bailey another T-Bonz to coax her into the van, and she made the high leap from the ground up onto my lap in a single bound, shattering any illusion that she was getting so old and feeble that her time was coming soon anyway.

"Good dog," I said, rewarding her with the T-Bonz.

I felt the warm, salty sandpaper of her tongue licking my hand, looking for another treat or maybe just a friend. I pulled my hand away. She licked my face. Maybe our last kiss. That made me cry a little bit, which, of course, just made her lick me more. I told myself it was just the salt from my tears. Dogs like salt. Everybody knows that.

"Down!" I finally said, not able to take it anymore. Bailey obediently lay down on the seat next to me, her puppy-dog eyes stabbing me in the heart.

"Good girl," I said with a sigh.

Why couldn't she be her usual impossible self today? This would all be so much easier if she would shit on the rug or something.

I started the van and gave Bailey another T-Bonz. Maybe if I was lucky she would get carsick on the drive upstate to the Mohawk and Hudson River Humane Society, where Cydney had arranged for the deed to be done. That would be a nice distraction. Compared to really dealing with the clusterfuck of emotions I had in my gut that day, dog vomit would have been a blessing.

And a nice bookend, too—on our very first road trip with Bailey, she ralphed nonstop from New York to Boston. Rose and I had just adopted her, just moved in together, and just gotten our first car together, "Goldie"—a used Ford Escort wagon with tacky gold paint and beige interior that I, oddly, remember as our favorite car. I guess because it was our first. It didn't have to haul any of the baggage that we have now. Our maiden voyage as a domestic unit began with Bailey finding Rose's bottle of Xanax while we were packing. Child-safe caps mean nothing to a jonesing pit bull. Within seconds, Bailey had consumed enough anti-anxiety medication to never have to worry about anything ever again.

"We're such bad dog parents!" Rose shrieked as I got the vet on the phone. He told us to immediately force-feed Bailey hydrogen peroxide to induce vomiting. Bailey, perhaps thinking it would help get her buzz on, eagerly lapped it up and five minutes later hurled the pills along with what was left of the child-proof cap and a healthy serving of half-digested chunks of beige kibble from breakfast. The hurling of the acrid, nutty-smelling beige stuff continued all the way from New York to Boston. There seemed to be more inside that dog than there was dog. I had been less than sold on

Goldie's beige interior when we bought the car, but now, clearly, it was a good call.

It was on that same maiden voyage as a domestic unit that we bought the old cauliflower farm—a simple, white, hundred-year-old farmhouse up in the Catskills with a few outbuildings on what was left of what had once been a large farm—six acres for the price of a studio apartment in Manhattan. It was a couple towns over from Rose's parents' place in Delhi.

"Isn't it your dream house?" Rose said breathlessly when we first saw the place.

"You know, I never got this far in the dream department, but I've got to admit, it looks pretty good," I said, hugging her. This was less than six months after our first kiss. We were on a blistering fast track to domestic bliss.

We named the old cauliflower farm "Bailey Farm" after Bailey the dog, who had, in turn, been named after George Bailey, Jimmy Stewart's character in my favorite movie, Frank Capra's *It's a Wonderful Life*. Being a devotee of Frank Capra's while I was in film school was kind of like being a big Pat Boone fan back in the '60s. The anti-cool. But for me, coming from a less-than-functional family, raised by my workaholic father and a mother so "out there" she made Shirley MacLaine look like Barbara Bush, nothing was more outré, more exotic than Capra's Americana.

Settling down with Rose didn't feel like settling. She was my ticket out of the unhappy family I grew up in. We were adventurers in a brave new world where family holidays were not to be dreaded—a place of warm, happy noise, not the cold silences of my youth. Bailey Farm was where we were planning to live out our Wonderful Life together—at least three nights a week. We would leave late

Friday afternoon and come back to the city early on Monday in time for work. Even though we lived there only part-time, the farm took up a full-time residence in my dreams of the life Rose and I were starting together. Something was in the water that came up cold and clear from our mountain well. I would spend long, happy days fixing things around the house, and Rose would cook me breakfast, lunch, and dinner. We were homesteading, putting down roots.

My parents were nothing but supportive of the move. "Now you can finally get all your crap out of our garage," I remember Mom saying, adding one more unpleasant memory to the pile of mementos that I took with me when I packed up all my stuff and installed it in my very own garage. Looking through it all, I was forced to agree with my mother's assessment—most of it was, in fact, crap. But among the musty college textbooks I'd kept in the earnest belief that I might someday need to refer to *Discovering Physical Geology* or *The Complete Works of George Bernard Shaw* and the old sports equipment and the *was-that-ever-my-size* uniforms from my undistinguished careers as both Little Leaguer and Boy Scout, there were also treasures:

Kiki, my former security blanket/best friend. Poor Kiki, now little more than a threadbare scrap, had been loved almost to death.

My old holster and cap pistols. I took aim at a squirrel contentedly stuffing his cheeks with an acorn on the gravel driveway leading up to my garage there at Bailey Farm and pulled the trigger. The flat click made me miss the SMACK—SMACK—SMACK the cap pistol made when I loaded it with those little rolls of red paper caps and pumped imaginary lead into all manner of boogeymen.

And finally, my old friends the Matchbox cars. We got into all kinds of trouble together back in the day. I would make splendid cities to drive through using my blocks and Legos. One time when I was eight years old, I refused to clean my room for three weeks.

"I am going out to dinner with your father, and if this room is not cleaned up by the time we get back, you will get a spanking," Mom said.

I had not yet had a spanking during my eight years on the planet and decided that it might be fun. I had seen spanking in a black-and-white movie once. The boy was made to lie across his father's lap, where he got ten strikes with an open hand, after which the father said soberly, "I'm sorry, but it was for your own good." I didn't see my dad actually spanking me, but I liked the idea of us doing something together, especially if it was for my own good.

That wasn't how it went down.

Mom returned from dinner, looking haughty and imperious in her fake ermine coat, to find me driving my Matchbox cars through the grand metropolis of blocks and Legos that I had erected on the blue and green carpet squares in my room as if our little predinner talk about getting a spanking had never happened.

Mom left the room soon to return not with Dad but with a wooden dowel three feet long and half an inch thick. I hadn't seen it before. Perhaps it had been set aside for just this purpose. It made a pleasing *whoosh* sound as it swung through the air, but the electric bite it had as it went *smack* against my thighs was like nothing I had ever felt before.

The blows came thick and fast as she chased me around my

room, *smack—smack—smack* on my bare legs as I ran around picking up my Matchbox cars in my Underoos. Meanwhile, Mom was shrieking, "I TOLD YOU TO CLEAN YOUR ROOM!"

I didn't know where Dad was during all this, except gone. Their dinner was over so he must have been home, but even when he was home, he could still be gone. He could disappear in plain sight when he wanted to, and I guess that night he wanted to because I didn't see him until the next morning when he appeared at my door to tell me that my mother wanted to speak to me.

"I cleaned my room!" I chirped. I had. It was spotless. The metropolis I had spent the last three weeks constructing was less than a memory; a regret. I wanted Dad to see that I had learned my lesson.

"Ah . . . looks good," he said, not looking at it, already on his way out the door. "Your mother just has some . . . some feelings that she wants to share with you."

He returned a moment later with Mom, pale and half-naked in her morning uniform of panties and an old white T-shirt. Mom inspected the welts on my leg with the pursed-lip concentration she gave all owies—the difference being, of course, that the angry red welts, now tinged purple from bruising, were ones she had given me. Mom shook her head and started to cry.

"I . . . I'm sorry, honey. I just . . . I just lost my head."

Looking back, I can see now that this apology was supposed to make me feel better, but at the time it just confused me. The only salve I'd had for the beating the night before was the idea that there was some rightness to the act. Spankings were "for my own good." I thought I had "learned a lesson," but instead Mom had just lost her head. Mom seemed to lose her head all the time, especially when things were going well. Especially holidays. So the lesson for me was that this beating could happen again at any time.

Mom sat on my bed and cried. She reached out tentatively to hug me, and I hugged her back for all I was worth. I thought if I could make Mom feel better, then she wouldn't lose her head and therefore not have to beat me. I looked up at Dad, and he smiled at me. He was proud of me. I had a done a good job. It was my job to take care of Mom so she wouldn't lose her head and have to beat me.

This was what I learned as a boy.

I SAT ON A STACK of my college textbooks in my garage at Bailey Farm, staring at the Matchbox cars, looking dusty and small at the bottom of one of the boxes I had taken from my parents' house. I couldn't believe that I still had those cars, that these keepsakes had actually been kept safe. This was back before our year from hell when I could still cry about things, and I cried about this.

I took those cars and I built a shelf for them, giving them a place of honor at Bailey Farm. Rose and I renovated every single inch of that farmhouse, sanding smooth the wide-plank pine boards of the floor, putting two coats of fresh paint on all its walls, patching the tall peak of its roof. Fixing up that house with Rose fixed up my life and renovated my heart. At Bailey Farm, I believed that we could make a home where our children's keepsakes would be mementos of family moments they actually wanted to remember, instead of moments they wished they could forget.

But then we'd sold Bailey Farm, the dream of the happy life we would make for our children upstate replaced by the reality of needing to pay for a roof over their heads in New York City.

And now Bailey, the dog that started it all, that bought that farm for us, was going to buy the farm.

ON THE WAY UPSTATE to the humane society, I kept giving Bailey the T-Bonz biscuits, which she seemed to like very much. This was disappointing. I was hoping they would make her throw up. I would have to stop to clean out the van. This would take time. Perhaps enough time for the humane society to close for the day. A reprieve.

Bailey, mouth dry from all the biscuits with nothing to wash them down, coughed and snorted and then started having one of those bouts of reverse sneezing dogs get where they snort and wheeze like they've swallowed an accordion. Promising. I wanted to throw up just looking at her. The attack finally subsided. Bailey stood very still for a moment.

And then, she farted.

Shoot. I couldn't brake for a mere fart.

Bailey's farts always sounded the same, like a chair pushing back on a wood floor, always exactly the same pitch and tone, call it a B-flat. And yet, in the everlasting now in which dogs lived, the fart always happened for the first time, always took Bailey by surprise. She would bow her brindle body, craning to look at her pink puckered tush to see if the sound might happen again. And then, losing interest or just forgetting what had brought her snout back to her haunch in the first place, she figured as long as she was there, she might as well lick herself, which was what she was doing now as we pulled up in front of the humane society.

Not a bad way to go, I guess.

I wanted to laugh, but it seemed that there was more crying to do.

"God, this just . . . *sucks*," I finally said, wiping my eyes.

I looked over at Bailey. "Sorry . . . I know it sucks worse for you."

"IT'S LIKE GOING TO SLEEP," Cydney said.

"Except she'll never wake up," I said.

"Yeah."

I just stared dumbly at her, which she took for my assent. She nodded to the veterinary technician to give Bailey the shot. "The shot." That's what they called it. Like this was just a routine trip to the vet's office to get a vaccination. Sodium pentathol. Truth serum, that's what they use to kill you. That killed me. One good shot of truth and you were done. Wham. *Done.*

The technician gave Bailey the shot.

She made that little sigh she always made when her legs were finally all tucked around her just right and she was going to grab some winks. I reached over and scratched her between her cock-eyed ears, gave her a good pat, making the dust motes dance in the splash of sunlight above her head. I would always remember the light of that summer we got Bailey. The light, or perhaps just the memory of it, was golden. Everything was just beginning for us. There was a wonderful sharpness to things. Rose and I were so vivid, in love, giddy in the thrilling ease of each other's bodies, each other's dreams. It was all happening. All at once.

Looking back now, it seemed that everything—the first kiss, moving in together, buying the farm upstate, adopting this poor, sweet, damaged dog—had happened in one impossibly hopeful, sun-dappled, forever-now instant of time that we thought would never end.

"How much time do we have?" I asked Cydney as I cradled Bailey in my arms.

"I'm sorry, she's already gone."

Chapter Seven

VICKSBURG

"**W**ORLD'S LONGEST-RUN-NING MELODRAMA!**"**
Next to the "Please Wait to Be
Seated" sign in the Vicksburg, Mississippi, Applebee's was a rack of
tourist brochures. While I waited for the hostess to seat Dad and
me for dinner, I checked out the one for *The World's Longest-
Running Melodrama*. According to the brochure, the Vicksburg
Theatre Guild had been presenting *Gold in the Hills, or The Dead
Sister's Secret*, continuously since March 28, 1936, which made it,
according to the *Guinness World Records*, the world's longest continuously running melodrama. If only we'd known they kept records
for continuous melodrama, we could have invited the Guinness
people over for one of our family's holiday dinners and given the
Vicksburg Theatre Guild a run for their money. Our semiannual
family gatherings often had a bad community-theater quality to
them, none of us really knowing where to stand or what to say.

And now Rose and I were carrying on that fine theatrical tradition.

"You *promised* that the renovations would be 100 percent done!" Rose yelled at me on my cell phone after Dad and I had been seated.

"I'll have the surf and turf," I said, not to Rose, but to our wait-person, Nancy. "It's just a little delay. Maybe the renovation will still be done in time," I said to Rose. "Can I get a salad with that?"

"Are you listening to me? *Maybe* doesn't help if you have asthma," Rose said.

"Don't you have an inhaler for that?"

"What kind of dressing do you want with your salad, hon?" Nancy asked.

"Um . . . dressing . . . ah . . . "

"I can't believe that you're not taking any responsibility for this!"

"What am I supposed to take responsibility for? The air conditioning contractor is the one who should have known in advance if we needed a new breaker box."

"Well, you're the one who hired him!"

"I can come back for the rest of your order . . . "

"No, ah . . . Italian's fine," I said, handing Nancy the menu. "Nick came well recommended and he's giving us a good price," I intoned in my best reasonable-husband voice.

"And what kind of potato, sugar?" I wanted to live at Applebee's. I just loved how they called everybody "sugar" or "honey"—it made the world a sweeter place.

"I can't believe you're taking his side over me!"

"Taking his side?"

"This box thing should have been known about before this happened!"

"So, not being able to predict the future—that's what I'm guilty of?!" This came out much louder than I'd intended. Now almost every "sugar" and "honey" in the place knew all about the domestic drama playing out at Table 12.

"Don't try to turn this around on me! It's not my fault I have a careless husband!"

"Well, you're the one who married me!"

I slammed my phone down on the table and then looked up to see that Dad and Nancy—and just about everybody else in the restaurant—were now staring at me. Finally, Nancy cleared her throat and said, "Sir?"

"I'm sorry, terribly sorry, I'll, ah . . . keep it down."

"Sir?"

"I said I'll keep it down, okay? Do you want me to leave?"

"Sir, I was just wanting to know what kind of potato you wanted with your surf and turf."

"Oh, ah . . . um . . . fries, please. Thank you."

"Yes, sir," Nancy said, walking away. I wasn't her sugar anymore.

I took a long pull on my beer. *"Careless husband,"* Rose had called me. That was one that pushed my ape-shit button. Rose had this preternatural ability to think ahead and was continuously surprised at the world's inability to keep up with her. I remember sitting in the IKEA cafeteria back before Sam was born, congratulating myself on thinking to get five extra clear plastic Samla storage boxes for all the baby stuff, and Rose saying, "After we finish here, we should go to Babies R Us to get his winter clothes." We'd just found out that our Sam was going to be a Sam and not a Samantha. I'd lobbied for waiting to find out until he/she was born, but there were important things, like shopping, to be considered.

"Haven't you already purchased his wardrobe for his entire first year?" I pointed out, shoving more Swedish meatballs in my mouth.

"Yes, but the winter clothes are on sale *now,* and he's going to be a spring baby, so if we wait until he needs his second-year winter clothes to buy them, we'll be behind the sale cycle and have to pay full price." Rose said this like it was the most obvious thing in the world.

I think it was her ability to think ahead like this that made our year from hell hit her so hard—she never saw it coming. She'd gone from being a person who was two steps ahead her entire life to flat on her back.

"You okay?" Dad asked as I sipped my beer.

I nodded and then, as I am prone to do when things really aren't funny, I told a joke: "Been a while since we had a good scene in a restaurant. It's almost like Mom's here." Dad was kind enough to laugh.

My mother's theatrics were legend in many a fine eating establishment near our home. She played birthdays, weddings, and, memorably, my father's retirement dinner. For the entire holiday season between Thanksgiving and Christmas, you could almost always count on dinner and a show. Mom's last great performance as our dinner-theater diva happened before Benny was born, back when Sam was just two. The venue was the sort of overpriced, atmosphere-free hotel restaurant that Dad learned to pick in later years—the kind of anonymous place that seemed more suited to meeting a mistress than making memories. That way if Mom made a scene, what happened at the Marriott stayed at the Marriott. The service was routinely awful the way it is at places that automatically add the gratuity to parties of six or more.

The waiter felt the wrath of Mom.

"Why's it taking so long? Did they have to kill the cow before they cooked it?!" Mom intoned with her trademark scenery-chewing flair, making heads turn in the restaurant. The poor waiter spoke just enough English to understand that he was being insulted, but not enough to defend himself.

"I . . . Mrs., I will immediately please check on cow, I mean dinner for you," he said and ran away. Mom could be that scary. Especially back in her prime.

She brought the house down at my wedding. I'd been dining out on my crazy mama stories for years, and many of our friends were eager to meet the legend in the flesh. One of Rose's bridesmaids, a TV actress of some renown as a dinner-party diva herself, couldn't resist challenging my mother to a duel—sniping at five paces.

"Mrs. Millhone, it is *such* a pleasure to meet you. I've heard so many *interesting* things about you."

Mom sized up her opponent and then said, "Oh, I know you. You're an actress or something. I have to say, you're much more attractive in person than I would've thought from seeing you on TV."

Mom had a black belt in backhanded compliments. Rose's bridesmaid just stood there in a slack-jawed standing eight-count until Mom finished her off with, "Well, enjoy your fifteen minutes," and walked away.

Even though Mom had lost a step or two since the wedding and had to rely on an oxygen tank to manage strenuous tasks like going to the store to buy more cigarettes, she still knew how to make a grand exit, flicking the clear breathing tube of her oxygen tank like a lion tamer cracking a whip. It was something to behold.

The tension was building that night at the Marriott.

"Your foods will be ready in just a few more of minutes," our nervous waiter said while Mom glared at him.

My older brother Kirk, handsome in an everyday, Midwestern kind of way, the tallest of the three Millhone "boys" and won't let you forget it, tried to lighten the mood, entertaining us by laughing at his own jokes. This was the happy Kirk, all bluster and bonhomie, heroically shouldering the burden of making conversation for all of us, keeping the silence at bay. I genuinely appreciated it. A corporate consultant, Kirk got paid to talk and did it well. But when he felt his services were not being properly appreciated, he was quick to pick up his toys and go home.

His daughter Casey sat on his lap, but it was hard to tell who was clinging to whom; he held her like a shield, as if her smiling face and pigtails could protect him from the fusillade of unhappy memories unleashed whenever all of us get together. I was doing the same thing with Sam.

In attempting to quantify the emotional fallout of growing up in our less than functional family, Kirk would refer to the concentric circles used to chart the effects of nuclear fallout. Me, the youngest by a gap of nine years, he would place on the outer rim of the emotional destruction; I'd gotten only a glancing blow. (It seemed that, even in my dysfunction, I didn't quite measure up.) Kirk, the middle child, placed himself in the middle circle of the emotional fallout. It had burned a large hole in him that he'd tried to fill with accomplishments. He was a world-record-holding, *summa cum laude* Eagle Scout with extra merit badges, but whether all that was enough to fill the hole, only he can say.

If Kirk was in the middle of the fallout, Paul, the oldest, was at ground zero. Paul had never quite admitted he wasn't the tallest. He was wearing one of his Orvis shirts that night, both UV and mosquito repellent. An unusual fashion choice for fine dining, but it totally worked on Paul. Since he didn't have a nuclear family unit of his own to shield him from his unhappy memories like Kirk and I did, I bet if HAZMAT made formal wear, Paul would've worn the suit to our semiannual family dinners.

He'd cut himself off from the family so many times that he sometimes felt more like a phantom limb than like my brother. A year could pass without hearing from him. He'd lost almost everything in the Northridge earthquake of '94. His apartment building was condemned, and the restaurant where he worked as an executive chef closed down. He spent a month sleeping in Red Cross shelters and the back of his pickup truck. Through it all, he told everyone he was "fine," upholding our fine Midwestern tradition of denial.

Paul had spent the last five years matriculating at a two-year community college in Los Angeles, taking almost every course they offered and even teaching a few. You learned to be wary of his encyclopedic intelligence. If you touched upon one of the many topics on which Paul's speed-reading had rendered him an expert, having a conversation with him was like drinking from a fire hose.

When the food finally arrived, Mom turned up her nose and stormed out. (An impressive task for a woman in her seventies carrying an oxygen tank for her emphysema.) This was all part of the show. Dad waited the usual amount of time and then excused himself to go after her.

My brothers and I looked down at the table, trying not to smile. Strangely enough, moments like this weren't what caused tension in my family. Just the opposite. They allowed us to exhale—the other shoe had finally dropped. I felt more relaxed than I had since sitting down at the restaurant. And closer to my brothers. This was familiar; this we knew. These uncomfortable silences were *ours* in the way other families had baseball or summer vacations on the Cape.

Dad came back without Mom.

"Well, she couldn't have gotten far," Kirk said. "Old ladies can't run."

Rose volunteered to check the ladies room—no dice. Dad wandered off again, real concern knitting his brow for the first time. I stopped smiling. My brothers and I looked at each other.

"Well, you don't see me going after her," Kirk said. That, to his mind, would be rewarding Mom for bad behavior. Tough love—and if you don't like it, tough luck. That's how he rolls.

"What about you?" I asked Paul.

"I'm really enjoying this steak," he said with a shrug.

As usual, it was up to me.

Leaving Sam with Rose, I went on the Mom hunt. Kirk was right, Mom couldn't have gotten far. She usually just stepped out for a smoke. But finding the nearest exit proved difficult—our hotel restaurant was "conveniently located" within a disorienting maze of interconnected shopping malls. I avoided all stairways as Mom's bad lungs and unsteady gate would make them treacherous, and I thought she would avoid them. Finally, having walked farther than her old legs could have possibly taken her, I circled back, taking a shortcut across the sweltering parking lot, and found Mom right outside the Marriott, puffing away, portable oxygen at the ready should she inhale too deeply. She decided to brave the stairs after all. I sat down next to her.

"Don't see why this is causing such havoc. Everybody ought to know I have my . . . episodes by now," she said.

"We just got concerned when Dad couldn't find you."

Her hand shook as she took a drag on her cigarette.

"Come on, Mom, it's hot out here. Let's go back."

She started to cry. "I don't know if I could make it back up the stairs."

She was old and she was lame and she was sick—having persisted at feeling sorry for herself for so long, life had finally rewarded her with things really worth feeling sorry about. Her ability to spoil everything, to pop any bubble of holiday family feeling had always been the thing that I hated most about my mother, but somehow I couldn't begrudge her anymore. Spoiling everything was now, perhaps, her only form of recreation. Who was I to stand in the way of one of the few things that still gave her pleasure?

I told Mom I loved her and stroked her back just the way she used to stroke mine when I was a baby. She was so skinny that I could feel each and every vertebra in her back, the tendons that fastened onto her shoulder, and the knobs of her collarbones poking through her thin shirt. I knew that all this was, to some degree, a game. This was what she'd wanted from the start: to get her pets, to be special—if only in her pitifulness.

I played into it. Rewarded her bad behavior. Things I would

never do for my child, I indulged in for her as our roles became ever more reversed. Children can be taught, but this old girl had only her few tricks left and not much time remaining to play them out. She was just trying to find her peace, that's all. That's what she said. It occurred to me that Mom finding her peace would be like a dog catching its tail. If it ever happened, what would she do with it?

Dad finally showed up and patted me on the back for doing this thing he could not do. My father dealt with my mother and her "episodes," as she called them, by *not* dealing, by avoiding her. This scene at a restaurant would become just one more thing for us not to talk about, an echo of all the awkward silences that had come before. I had thought Rose was my ticket out of all that, but now that we'd gotten married and settled down, we were starting to have little silences of our own.

Growing like weeds.

"HELLO? ARE YOU THERE? HONEY?"

I could hear breathing but she didn't answer me. I lay back on the motel bed and stared up at the textured ceiling.

"Look, I'm sorry about before, when I was at the restaurant," I said. "I was just hungry and tired from driving all day. You know what a grumpus I am when I need to eat," I said with a laugh. Silence. Laughing alone is almost as lonely as drinking alone.

"And I'm sorry about the air conditioning thing. I know I promised that it would get finished by the time I got back from picking up this car. I told Nick, the AC guy, about your asthma and everything. He said he'd do his best."

Silence.

Apparently, Nick's best was not good enough for her. I was starting to think that mine wasn't either. As I held on to the phone, waiting in vain for this silence to thaw, I pictured Rose, remembering how she'd looked at me when I dropped her and the boys off at her parents' place in upstate New York before beginning my descent into Dallas to fetch this used car that I somehow imagined was going to give us a new life. After I hugged and kissed the boys good-bye, I saw Rose just looking at me, her head tilted slightly to one side. I couldn't get past that look of hers—the almost-squint in which she tried to fix me, as if her eyes were tired from the astigmatism of two competing images of me: the man she thought she had married (and the life she thought she would have) versus the man that was standing before her at this crossroads in our lives. It was that guarded, unhappy look that I had come to resent more than anything. Words can be taken back, actions apologized for, but there was no denying the unhappiness in her eyes. I think men can forgive anything but unhappiness. I don't mean that men stop loving women because they make them unhappy—if that were true, what would poets write about all day? But failing to bring happiness to the woman we love, that injures a man's heart too deeply for any of us to long endure.

"Hello?"

Silence.

"So, we're not talking now, is that it?" I asked.

She said nothing but I heard her loud and clear.

Nothing is louder than the sound of not talking.

Chapter Eight

MUSIC CITY, USA

"**C**AN I DRIVE?**"** Dad asked as we checked out of our Motel Six, just a strip mall away from the Applebee's where I had carried on our fine family tradition of making scenes in restaurants the night before.

"You want to drive the Bomber?" I asked Dad.

"Why should you get to have all the fun?"

I tossed him the keys over the top of the car. Very Starsky and Hutch. We got in.

"You adjust the side mirror with that thingy there," I said, giving Dad a quick tour of the Blue Beckham Bomber's cockpit. "Here's the lights . . . the seat adjuster thingy is down here . . . go easy on the accelerator until you get used to the car; the Bomber's got quite a kick."

"Yes, Dad," my father said with a wink, starting the car.

"Make sure you look both ways before pulling out of the parking lot," I said, only half-pretending to mother hen; men can be new-baby-precious about new cars.

"I taught *you* how to drive, remember?" Dad said, smirking.

"I can't believe you made me learn how to drive on a *Ford Tempo*. That's like having your first kiss be with your Aunt Eunice or something." Few will remember the Ford Tempo, and those who do will not mourn its passing. The perfect car in which to commit a crime: no distinguishing features whatsoever, like driving a limp handshake.

"We got a good deal on that car," Dad said.

"I bet you did," I cracked. "They were desperate to get it off the lot."

If depression were a color, it would look like the Tempo's exterior: a dull, dishwater gray. It also sported blood-red accent stripes that looked like someone had run over a squirrel and then rubbed the roadkill's bushy tail down each side of the car. Inside this fine vehicle: roadkill-red vinyl interior to match. I spent the first hangover of my life in the backseat of that car. The morning after I discovered the fine game of quarters my freshman year of high school, my parents, in a sneak attack of normalcy, suggested that we do something family-oriented on a weekend. At that time, we lived in the Arlington, Virginia, of cemetery fame, and my parents picked that particular morning to insist that we take the new Tempo across the Potomac River for a nice Sunday drive taking in the sights of our nation's capital.

"Why couldn't I have finished learning to drive on the Saab?" I said.

"You drove the Saab?"

"No, but Mom used to let me shift for her. Guess I was nine or ten."

"I didn't know that."

"You weren't around."

Dad nodded loudly—he's always loudest when there's something he's not saying. I sighed loudly, just adding to the din of things unsaid. I felt for my dad, could see in the way his squint narrowed as he scanned the road ahead that he was hurting.

It's not so much that I have painful memories of my father growing up. I have good memories, actually. It's just that I needed a lot more of them.

Playing with Matchbox cars is one of the few things I remember us doing together. Dad would come home from work, loosen his tie, and we would hunker down on the carpet of my room to play "Joe" and "Mr. Peacock." Joe and Mr. Peacock would do all sorts of interesting work together. Make roads for the Matchbox cars to drive on. Build houses out of blocks for all the imaginary Matchbox people to live in. Joe never had to miss his old buddy Mr. Peacock when Mr. Peacock had to go to work because Joe and Mr. Peacock worked together. I liked that. But one day Mr. Peacock just stopped showing up to work with Joe. No explanation, no doctor's note. He was just gone. Joe tried to carry on without Mr. Peacock, but it wasn't the same.

I know that Dad missed playing Joe and Mr. Peacock too because one fine Sunday afternoon when I was fourteen and the deal with the family therapist was that Dad had to make time for quality time, he tried playing Joe and Mr. Peacock with me again.

"Say, Joe, do you think that speedboat over there is going to come our way?" he said from the back of the canoe he'd rented for our family–therapist–mandated quality time that day. I stopped paddling and rolled my eyes with epic peeve the way only a fourteen-year-old can.

"Did you just, like, try to play *let's pretend* with me? That was fun when I was, like, four, but in case you haven't noticed, I'm *fourteen* now!"

"Sorry," Dad said and that was all. He never tried to play Joe and Mr. Peacock with me again. Never tried to make me go canoeing again either. Fine by me at the time because, like most teenage boys, I would much rather spend my Sunday afternoons alone in my room so I could pick my zits and masturbate in peace.

WE STOPPED FOR GAS. I filled up the Bomber's tank at the pump while Dad emptied his in the men's room. These pit stops would be more frequent, he had warned me, now that the doctors had implanted radioactive seeds in his prostate to control the cancer. "The" cancer he always called it. Adding "the" made it sound singular, as if there was only one discrete cancer instead of millions of cells eating out his insides. I had trouble visualizing the radioactive seeds, burning down there where the sun doesn't shine, little bits of death that were keeping him alive. Maybe because the possibility that my father might be mortal had never occurred to me. Except for being a bit deaf in one ear—which I regarded, in Darwinian terms, as a necessary biological adaptation for surviving in the hostile environment of my mother's harsh words—Dad had always been almost preternaturally healthy. In his fifties, when most people are starting to slow down, he took up marathon running.

But he seemed suddenly fallible in the wake of the triple-whammy of his retirement, my mom's death, and cancer all in the span of six months. One morning, his hand slipped while he was trimming his beard, and he decided it best to shave off the rest so it could grow back evenly. His bushy, mountain-man's beard had been a permanent fixture on his face for my entire life. His naked chin looked so vulnerable. It was like Samson got a haircut.

Dad told me he was fine, not to worry about the cancer. He didn't want to make a "big deal about it." But that would be true even if—or, perhaps, especially if—he'd been afraid he was going to die. That was Dad. When I told Rose, who comes from a family of doctors, about Dad's cancer, in approximately five minutes she had an appointment for him to get a second opinion from a preeminent cancer specialist. That was Rose.

I'm grateful for my father's cancer. Grateful that, knock wood, it was treatable but also grateful that he got it. Adversity has its blessings. This little speed bump made Dad slow down and smell the roses a little bit and made me realize that he wasn't going to be around forever; so if I had any plans for giving him a second chance, the sooner the better.

Dad came back from the bathroom and I got in the shotgun seat again, giving him another turn at the wheel. As we merged onto the road again, I said, "Dad, about before when I was talking about driving with Mom and everything and you not being around and stuff, I didn't mean to make you feel bad . . . "

"No," he said. "You're right, I . . . I wasn't around."

I sighed. "Well . . . you're here now."

Dad smiled in a way that made me want to cry.

"So, how do you like driving the Bomber?" I said to change the subject. Being this comfortable with my father was something I wasn't quite comfortable with yet.

"Oh, it's a hell of a car."

"You really think so? I know it's not a Prius."

"Here's what I love about this car . . . "

He pulled up behind the car in front of us, eased into the passing lane, and then put the hammer down. You wouldn't think my old dad would have that much lead in his foot, but man, did he roll that day. The Bomber just purred, butter-smooth, not breaking a sweat. The car we passed was all of a sudden just *gone*, less than a memory.

"You gotta love that," I said.

"Vroooooom," Dad growled in agreement. He was like a little kid playing with a really big Matchbox car.

Joe and Mr. Peacock ride again.

THE ROAD STRETCHED OUT BEFORE US, content to have its curves straightened. We were on the Natchez Trace Parkway, as pretty a stretch of road as you are likely to find east of the Mississippi. We were bound for Nashville—Music City, USA.

And we were singing.

A beer song from my father's misspent youth. He sang the verses and I joined him for the chorus.

> I wish all the girls were like fish in the ocean
> If I were a shark, I'd show them some motion!
> Oh roll your leg over, oh roll your leg over,
> Oh roll your leg over the man in the moon.

I wish all the girls were like Hansel and Gretel,
If I was old Hansel, I'd mettle with Gretel!
Oh roll your leg over, oh roll your leg over,
Oh roll your leg over the man in the moon.

I wish all the girls were like B-29s,
If I was a fighter, I'd buzz their behinds!
Oh roll your leg over, oh roll your leg over,
Oh roll your leg over the man in the moon.

Every now and again this irrepressibility comes over my father in the form of song. He'll be working on the house, in the yard, something with his hands, and he'll just start belting one out. He hams up the whole thing, unleashing his inner Pavarotti, gesturing grandly with his hands, throwing his head back for the high notes and always with a little smile on his face that says he knows *exactly* how silly and off-key the whole ruckus is; but, until the song is over, he just doesn't give a damn.

It's so beautiful when it happens. Like a flower that blooms only once every seven years.

"Here's another one," Dad said, on a roll. "There used to be this jingle for Pepsi-Cola, and my Sunday school teacher rewrote it."

Christianity hits the spot,
Twelve Apostles, that's a lot.
The Holy Ghost and the Virgin, too,
Resurrection! It's the thing for you!

We laughed and then just drove on for a while, getting lost in the windshield. Dad started to hum again and eventually broke into an old Mills Brothers tune. He was still behind the wheel, but part of

him was miles away and fifty years ago, holding my mother in his
arms for the first time.

> Since first I saw the love light
> In your eyes
> I thought the world
> Held not but joy for me
> And even though
> We've drifted far apart
> I never dream
> But what I dreamed of you
>
> I love you
> As I never loved before
> Since first I saw you on the village green
> Come to me
> Or my dream of love is all
> I love you
> As I loved you
> When you were sweet
> When you were sweet sixteen

After that, it was quiet in the car, just the purr of the engine and
the hum of the tires. It was grand to finally have a silence with my
father filled not with things unsaid but, instead, with things that
didn't need to be.

I missed Mom, too.

Chapter Nine

TRAIL OF TEARS

WE STOPPED for gas again and switched drivers before motoring up the rest of the Natchez Trace Parkway to Nashville. The Natchez Trace, like many historic routes, began as an animal path through the forest. Funny to think that in driving on this historic road we were following in the footsteps of some wild pig that went a-wandering, looking for a shortcut to the watering hole. History, at least the user-friendly variety that you read about in books, seems to be as much about forgetting as remembering. One chapter in the Natchez Trace's history that must be remembered because many would rather forget it is that the Trace was on the route of the "Trail of Tears," the forced relocation in 1838 of the Cherokee Indians from their ancestral home in the rapidly gentrifying American Southeast to a reservation in a more low-rent neighborhood west of the Mississippi.

As we drove along the Trace, I wondered if there was a Trail of Tears museum someplace along our route and, if so, if it had a gift shop. I needed souvenirs for Sam and Benny—cheap priceless things for them to gleefully fish from my pockets upon arrival. I wouldn't be surprised if they had *Trail of Tears* key chains, *Trail of Tears* die-cast metal tractor-trailer toy sets, maybe even *Trail of Tears* commemorative shot glasses and beer cozies. In the cultural life of a nation, gift shops seem to represent closure. You know you've really put the past behind you when you're ready to use it to sell souvenirs.

I shook my head, wondering if I would ever get even a cheap T-shirt's worth of closure on my mother's death. A souvenir ashtray might be more appropriate to commemorate a lifetime spent puffing her life away.

I looked over at Dad, drowsing next to me in the shotgun seat, and remembered getting the call from him, just three days after they celebrated their fiftieth anniversary. Somehow I just knew it was "the call" the moment I picked up the phone. Could just hear it in the soft hiss of phone silence after I said, "Hello?"

"It's your dad. I, ah . . . I needed to tell you that your mother's in the hospital. Carole, she, ah . . . complained of feeling very tired last night. This was after dinner about seven o'clock and then, ah . . . she had some . . . some pain in her chest and, ah, I thought, well, best to have her looked at and what have you and so I called an ambulance and they took her to the . . . the emergency room at the Virginia Hospital Center and, ah . . . the doctors looked at her and it was, um, fairly clear that she had a . . . a heart attack. Just a question of . . . how serious and to tell that they had to, ah, do some tests and what have you but she was . . . she was resting quite comfortably and was awake and her mind was sharp and she seemed . . . seemed stable. By this time it was quite late, past one a.m., and so

I went home to try to rest and then I . . . I got a call early this morning. She lost, ah . . . consciousness, ah . . . at some point during the . . . the night and . . . and . . . "

He seemed to grind to a halt. It was quiet for a moment and then there was a sound I'd never heard before.

The sound of my father crying.

"I think she might not make it," he finally said, voice cracking with the strain of uttering these words.

I stood in our kitchen with the phone pressed to my ear, nodding, even though he wasn't saying anything. Not for the moment. Just coughing, collecting himself. I stared at the dry-erase bulletin board next to the phone. Noticed the mussed phone number of a college chum that I had always meant to call. The menu for our favorite Chinese place tacked next to it. The mess of life is just so insensitive, so insistent. When you're hearing that your mother just had a massive heart attack, there should be a reprieve, one shouldn't be bothered with the question of why do we keep the damn take-out menu when we always order the same thing?

My mom was dying.

The fact of that was there, burning hot, but it was like I was staring at it through dark sunglasses. I felt cold inside. I was saying something to Dad, something about when I could leave to drive down there, but my voice sounded far off, a stranger's, like this wasn't happening to me. I didn't feel sad. Or worried. Or much of anything at all. A breaker got tripped. The body protects itself, shuts down the emotion circuit when it gets overwhelmed so the whole system doesn't crash. I knew this feeling. This necessary numbness. For a second it was like I was right back in the Intensive Care Unit with Benny, hour-by-hour, no sleep for five days, time stopped, no day no night, just the *beep, beep, beep* of the vital signs monitor, living and dying in the eternity between each breath, please God don't let it be his last.

That feeling again. That block of ice in my gut.

Just two months after Benny made his bumpy landing in this world, Mom was taking off from it. Just like an airport. Arrivals and Departures.

"I would arrive, let's see . . . " I heard myself say, almost surprised to find the phone still in my hand, Dad still on the line. "Depends upon traffic. If I leave right away, I can avoid rush hour here, make it down in about four hours or so."

"Okay. Kirk has to fly from Minneapolis and Paul is in Los Angeles, so I doubt they'll make it in before tomorrow. I should go. You've got my cell number?"

"Yeah. But they make you turn off your phone in the ICU, so I won't be able to reach you. But don't worry, I'll be fine."

I'll be fine.

As I hung up the phone, the sad fact of knowing this wore upon me. I had discovered during our all-too-recent experience with Benny that I had a certain gift for personal tragedy. I was great in hospitals. I knew to turn off my cell phone, how to read the vital signs monitor, and how to implode quietly instead of falling apart.

"Are you going to be okay driving?" Rose asked as I hung up the phone.

"Sure."

"Do you need me there?"

"I'll be fine."

"I could come down."

"What about the kids?"

"I could call my mother."

"I don't think there's time . . . "

I shook my head, momentarily stunned by the reality of this.

"Honey, are you okay?"

"I'm fine."

Rose hugged me. "But I want to be there for you."

"Thanks, honey."

"Families should all be together at times like this."

"We will be. But the kids are still at school, and I need to get down there before . . . "

I couldn't complete this sentence.

"Are you sure you're okay to drive?"

"Yes."

I sighed, opening my closet. What clothes do you pack to watch your mother die? Do you pack everything or nothing, not even a toothbrush? I opted for a change of clothes, dark, with extra T-shirts, underwear, and socks to extend as needed. Basic toiletries. A couple PowerBars, a banana, and a Diet Coke for the drive down. It was such a relief to pack, to give my brain these small hard-and-fast details to fix upon. I congratulated myself on being the kind of guy who could think to put Boomer's dog food in a Tupperware container at a time like this. I needed him for this trip, the comfortable doggy bulk of him—a walking throw pillow. I grabbed his leash and he wagged over to me, tail propelling him across the room.

Rose hugged me at the door, tearful in a way that I oddly envied. I was vaguely aware that I was not myself. Not the man she married. She had fallen in love with a guy who could cry at movies, and now I had no tears, not even for my mother.

Life does things to you, not all of them good.

"What should I tell the kids?" she said, finally releasing me.

"Tell them everything's fine."

"Everything's *fine*?"

I almost laughed. It was so what my father would say at a time like this.

A FULL TANK OF GAS: FORTY DOLLARS.

Getting yourself killed racing to your mother's deathbed: priceless.

"You fucking Subaru asshole dickweed motherfucker!" I yelled out the window, in full-on road rage, at some kid who'd cut in front of me in rush hour traffic along that nightmare stretch of I-95 that's all chemical plants and places to dump dead bodies.

The fucking Subaru asshole dickweed motherfucker rolled down his window and was kind enough to show me his brand-new baseball bat and his command of his middle finger. Boomer yelped, nervous.

I slowed down, giving the fucking Subaru asshole dickweed motherfucker and his baseball bat a wide berth. I patted Boomer on the head and thought about Mom.

It was just so passive-aggressive of her to die right now.

Right after our big argument. I had told her to go to hell, and three days later she was on her deathbed. If she kicked, not only would I get to feel guilty for the end of her miserable life but for her miserable *afterlife*, too.

It was just so *her*.

The argument took place just three days prior, when the whole family had been in town for my parents' fiftieth wedding anniversary. It concerned the subject of child-rearing. While I was reading bedtime stories to the boys, Mom took it upon herself to share with Rose certain tips she thought helpful in containing the natural rambunctiousness of young boys. While I acknowledge my mother's expertise at squashing the spirit of young boys, I took great exception to her lecturing Rose so pointedly about how she should be raising our children that it brought Rose to tears. It pushed a button in me, deploying the same cold, calculating fury that neutralized Bailey after recognizing the dog as a potential threat to our family. Mom needed to be neutralized.

"I just spoke my mind," Mom said in her defense when I confronted her at the kitchen table after the boys were asleep. "I should be able to speak my mind in my own house." I didn't listen to her defense. I was judge, jury, and executioner. My verdict was final.

"Your house—*my* kids," I said coldly, getting Mom in my crosshairs. "I'll make you a deal: I won't tell you how to decorate your house, and you don't pretend you're the mother of the year."

"Well, I still know a thing or two. I raised you, didn't I?"

"I raised myself. Dad was gone and you were nuts."

Bull's-eye.

Mom brought her spindly too-blue fingers to her face as if my words had physically struck her. For a moment all I could hear was her croaky breathing, the inhalator tube for her oxygen tank now so constant a feature in her face that I'd stopped noticing it. She exhaled through pursed lips; just sitting upright was like doing cardio for her.

I regretted what I said the moment after I said it. Especially because it was true. I had made it a rule not to have any more honest conversations with my mother. It seemed like the loving thing to do. I took no pleasure in beating up an old lady. I had carried emotional baggage about my mother my whole life; I could carry it the rest of hers.

Finally, Mom shook her head and then, in a voice of infinite fatigue, said, "Well . . . I guess I botched it." Her eyes, now wet with tears, wandered as she said this, like she was reviewing not just the day's events but all the days of her life that led to this cruel moment—having me, her baby, the one she could always talk to, tell her that all she'd ever been and all she'd ever tried to be for him was null and void. Negligible. A botched job.

This was my last conversation with my mother.

WHEN I GOT TO THE HOSPITAL, Dad was sitting in a chair next to Mom's bed in the Intensive Care Unit. He looked up at me and smiled in that terribly sad way that only Midwesterners can: bearing up, making do, accommodating death as politely as we would any other unanticipated houseguest. I sat down next to him.

"I hope you weren't planning to be strong for me here because I was really kind of planning to get through this by being strong for you," I said.

We smiled each other's sad smile and then turned to look at what was left of Mom. Her face looked bloated, foreign.

"The nurse told me it's from the medication," Dad said, almost hopefully, as if this was somehow a healthy sign. I, unfortunately, knew my way around an Intensive Care Unit; knew what each of the tubes and wires were for; what the numbers on the vital signs monitor meant. Her blood pressure dipped slowly downward . . . 85/50 . . . 72/39 . . . as the Fed Ex trucks carrying oxygen in her bloodstream hit more and more speed bumps. There is a momentum to death that speeds up as your ticker winds down. As the heart muscle dies and stops properly circulating oxygen, the other tissues of the body begin to die as well. Death is rarely one moment, but like most annoying things about life, it is "a process." That's why death is something that must be declared.

Dad had excused himself, to get some food he said, but I expect just to cry, when I noticed that Mom's blood pressure had dipped to 50/25.

"I think we need to send somebody to get my dad," I told the nurse.

The nurse looked at the monitor and then called for an orderly.

"How long does she have?" Dad asked when he got back to Mom's bed.

"Well, let me just say that if we were to disconnect the pacemaker and take her off the ventilator, that she's at the point that her heart would stop beating," the nurse said. I wondered how many people she had seen die. How many final moments had passed through her hands? She was really good at it. I admired her answer to the question of how much time my mother had, the way she gently eased Dad into the fact that they weren't saving her life anymore, just prolonging it. Her work was largely done with Mom. We were her patients now.

"If you'd like, I can clean her up so you can spend some time with her without all these machines in the way," she said.

I looked at Dad, his always-watery blue eyes dripping slow and steady like a faucet. He nodded finally. "Carole didn't want any . . . heroic measures." He said this with a slow wave of his hand, fingers cutting through the air to say what he could not bear to put into words.

"Okay, just give me a few minutes to get her ready for you." She pulled a curtain around the bed while Dad and I waited by the nurse's station for Mom to take her final bow. Dad and I looked at each other. The damp chill of grief that had slowly worked its way into our bones during this longest of days was replaced by a grief that was like stepping outside when it's twenty below and the cold smacks you in the face.

Dad sobbed.

"When I left her last night and we said good-bye, I didn't know that . . . that was . . . " He sobbed again. I put an arm around Dad's shoulders and he, around mine. We just stood like that, holding each other up until the nurse pulled the curtain back.

"Take as much time as you need."

Dad and I advanced slowly, each taking one of my mother's graceful, long-fingered hands. I made myself look at her face, to see the death in the slackness of her lips, the bloat of her neck as the blood began to pool. I needed to see that she was dead, to understand what dead was, to really believe that she was not just sleeping.

Dad said something and I did too, but all I remember about our words was that they were unmemorable. Words fail you when you need them most; when you need them to say everything, they just fall on the floor like forgotten toys to be tripped over.

I remember holding my mother's hand, feeling the hand that had changed my diapers and fixed my dinner and felt my brow for fever and rubbed my back when I couldn't sleep slowly become cold meat in my hands.

Nothing, before or since, has ever felt so final.

Chapter Ten

NOT WYOMING

"**D**O YOU THINK that Mom knew that she was dying?" I asked Dad.

We were sitting in a booth at a truck stop somewhere in the Great Smokey Mountains near the Tennessee-Virginia border. He sipped the weak coffee, mulling.

"I think part of her did," he finally said. "When I said good-bye the night before Carole passed, I just said, 'Love you,' and she said, 'Love you' like it was any other good-bye. I thought I would just go home for a couple hours and see her in the morning . . . " His eyes grew misty, but he made no attempt to wipe the tears, to apologize. My father had gotten quite good at crying. When he had tears, he just had them. Unashamed. The way he sang with me in the car. Missing Mom had made him into the accessible, emotional man she had missed him being while she was alive. Irony, like variety, abounds in nature.

"But as I turned to go, she . . . she reached up and she pulled me to her and she said again, 'I *love* you, John.' That kiss just . . . meant so much to me."

He went home humming that kiss, thought she would recover, thought that kiss was their fresh start, a meet-cute for their golden years together. But then he came back to the hospital the next day to find out that he was wrong, that the kiss was their good-bye, that she had slipped away, never to resume consciousness, and that the someday his whole life had been banked on, when everything finally settled down, when he wasn't working and they could finally just love each other, was never going to happen.

But still, he had that kiss, that last kiss, and the finality of it made it all the more precious. He felt she knew, somehow, that this was it, or could be, and wanted to make sure that he knew that she loved him, to give him that one undisputed kiss in which all the anger, all the struggle and miscommunication of their often unhappy half-century together were forgotten, absolved, a detail; that she saw him, in one last, clear moment, for the good man that he was.

This was his reward. It says everything about the kind of man my father is that this was enough for him.

As quickly as the tears had come upon him, they were gone. He chased them away with cherry pie and weak coffee. He smiled at me, blue eyes shining, clumsily patted my hand.

"Love you, guy."

"I love you, too, Dad."

As he got up to pay the check, I sat staring at his pie crumbs on the well-worn diner plate and wondered why *he* got to cry in a truck stop and I didn't. Not that I really wanted to cry, but it occurred to me that maybe I needed to—my father was now more in touch with his emotions than I was.

My father.

I had not cried for my mother, not since the white-hot grief moment when they pulled the plug in the hospital. I barely slept that night. I stayed up wandering around my parents' house, taking pictures. I wanted to record with my camera all the places that my mother's touch could be seen in the house. She was so particular: the dishes on the shelf just so; her well-equipped purse slung over a kitchen chair; the stacks of New Age books by her bed; the ashes in her secret ashtray on the back steps. I took pictures of all these. Still lifes of her absence. Tomorrow my brothers would come, things would be moved, and the house would slowly start to forget her. Taking the pictures was a way of holding on to what was left of Mom after they took her body away.

MOM'S REMAINS WERE RETURNED to us a couple days later in an oak box the size of a loaf of bread but much heavier. As I held the box in the backseat of Dad's pine-green Honda Accord, I wondered whether it was the ashes or the box or just the occasion that made it so heavy. We were on our way to the, what exactly do you call this? The Scattering? That sounded vaguely violent, like we were dismembering Mom or something. "The Sprinkling" didn't work either. Maybe I was just hungry, but that sounded somehow doughnut related.

Mom's will had not indicated any particular place she wished to have her ashes scattered, which seemed particularly un-particular for Mom. But, I guess, believing in reincarnation as she did, she saw this lifetime's body as being kind of like a rental—which may explain why she didn't take better care of it. Dad briefly considered scattering Mom's ashes in Wyoming. We have a small piece of property out there, and Dad planned to have his ashes scattered there when the time came. It was kind of a romantic notion, both of them up there on Sunlight Mountain, fertilizing the same pine trees together for all eternity. But it was kind of a schlep, especially with family and friends coming in for the memorial service the next day, and, as Dad pointed out, "Your mother hated Wyoming."

And so, here we were, driving around in Dad's Honda looking for a spot to do the deed. Dad wanted someplace nice, a natural setting overlooking the Potomac River. But someplace not too far away so he could go visit with Mom whenever he wanted to "commune with her energy." It was weird to have Dad say things like "commune with her energy." Mom always said lots of weird things like that, so, I don't know, maybe saying weird things was something Dad was doing to honor her. Kirk and Paul and I sort of looked at each other when he said it and made a collective—and quite rare—decision not to be smart-asses. It's what Mom would have wanted.

"I think up here is good," Dad finally said, turning off the George Washington Memorial Parkway into a parking area for a nature preserve.

We got out. Dad took point, followed directly by Kirk, who's always so alpha I was surprised he wasn't trying to lead. Paul hung back, bringing up the rear—a choice to eschew the petty politics of pecking order, trying to assert a less competitive dynamic, which was the main way that Paul competed with Kirk. (It was a tribute to their brotherly bond that they had managed to keep these kinds of rivalries going strong into their fifth decade.) I was in the middle of this mess per usual and annoyed to still be carrying the box because I knew that they had decided that it must be important for me, as the youngest, to have the honor of carrying the ashes and so they were going to be big brotherly about it and trust me not to fuck it up.

Which, of course, I would.

It was hot and humid on our little nature walk. My hands had become all sweat-slippery and cramped from carrying the heavy little box. With each step, I became more certain that I would fumble it and be teased mercilessly by my brothers for the rest of my life. I still hadn't lived down the Brussels sprouts I tried to hide under my seat cushion back when I was eight years old.

We finally came to the end of the trail, deep in the green; a pocket of hush in which mosquitoes had gathered. One was biting my arm, but I didn't slap at it for fear that I might drop Mom in the process.

"Well?" Kirk said, seeing his role as consensus builder here.

Dad shook his head. "I wanted her to be able to see the river. I mean not actually see, you know, but . . . " Dad sputtered and shook his head.

"It's okay," Paul said, placing a hand on Dad's shoulder.

Kirk nodded and said, "We'll take her to the river, Dad."

I watched this exchange and it dawned on me, perhaps for the first time, that my brothers might actually be nice. I love my brothers and know them to be good men and would trust them with my life—but never to be nice. Paul, who, I have to say, is occasionally profound, once put it like this: "Our family had a love that transcended comfort—and didn't offer any."

Kirk took point as we went off-road, pressing further into the enveloping, mosquito-rich green of the trees. It was a relief to have him lead simply because Kirk, not stepping out in front, was not Kirk. Paul was now at his heels, which was where he always was, so that was good, too. Then came Dad, staring up at the spots of blue that peeked through the canopy of trees to make sure that they were getting larger, that we were getting closer to where the forest ended at the riverbank. That was the rational thing to do, and therefore Dad was still Dad. I trailed along behind all of them, stuck with Mom like always.

It was actually kind of a relief to know that even with Mom gone, our family issues would still live on.

We finally came to a clearing on the edge of a bluff overlooking the Potomac River. A beautiful spot. The four of us looked at the vista and then to each other and, as one, nodded.

The perfect place.

I lifted up the box, presenting it in a manner that I intended to be ceremonial or, at least, respectful, grateful that disaster had been averted. I had not dropped the box. I had brought Mom safely to her final resting place.

Dad nodded and I gently pulled at the top of the box to open it, but it wouldn't open. I traced the ornamental cap with my fingers, looking for a catch or a clasp. Finding none, I placed both thumbs underneath the cap and pushed a little harder. Still the box would not open.

Paul coughed. Kirk swatted a mosquito.

I yanked in vain at the box in a most non-funereal manner and then, shaking my head, flipped it over in my hands to solve the riddle of how to open it. Four bright brass screws secured the stout little box.

"Shit," I said. "Does anybody have a screwdriver?"

Dad fished in his pockets. "I've got a dime, we could—"

"No, it's Phillips . . . "

Unfortunately none of us had anything remotely resembling a Phillips screwdriver, not even Paul, who always had some new nerdy whatchamacallit in his pocket but had recently traded in his Leatherman pocket knife for a new GPS locator. He could give exact coordinates of where we were, quite literally, screwed, but that was all.

No amount of swearing or yanking or jamming of car keys could convince the bright shiny screws to release their grasp. Bashing the box open on a rock was briefly considered and then discarded as a violent gesture, not in the spirit of the proceedings.

"We'll just have to go get a screwdriver and then come back, I guess," Dad finally said, his shoulders slumping.

"Honestly, John, this is just Mickey Mouse!"

That's what Mom would have said. I could almost hear her reproaching him from inside the little oak box as I carried it back to the car. Our kingdom, if we had one, for a Phillips screwdriver.

By the time we hiked back through the woods, got back in the car, drove all the way home, got a screwdriver, and got back on the George Washington Memorial Parkway, we were all beyond spent. Dad pulled off at the first scenic overlook we came to and said, "Let's just do it here."

Not nearly as idyllic as the first spot, but much more accessible.

It would make it much easier for Dad to come out and commune with Mom's energy . . . and the energy of all the commuters whipping by on the George Washington Memorial Parkway.

Paul held the box while Kirk unscrewed the lid. No one said anything. We finally got the oak box open. Inside that was another plastic container, and inside that was a twist-tie bag, and inside that was, of course, Mom. Dad did the honors, dipping into the bag and casting Mom's ashes to the four winds. Unfortunately, the strongest wind was coming off the Potomac, and the blowback led to a fair amount of Mom's mortal remains ending up on Dad's pants. I remember seeing the dark gray smudge on Dad's faded jeans and looking forward to the day when the gift of forgetting would take this little mental snapshot with it.

A small memorial service was planned for the next day at my parents' house—well, I guess now it was just *my Dad's* house because Mom was, you know, dead. A thousand and one little changes like this percolate through your gray matter as your mind tries to wrap itself around the passing of a parent. It's almost physically disorienting, like someone came into your house while you slept and rearranged all your furniture. You keep bumping into things.

Like my mother's bean salad.

We were eating lunch back at the house after spreading her ashes, going over to-do lists for the memorial service the next day, when I realized that the bean salad I'd been stuffing in my pie-hole was my mother's bean salad, the last she would ever make. You can steal yourself for painful phone calls, but there's no defense against bean salad. You never see it coming. I briefly considered trying to save one last bite of it somehow. Maybe freeze it. But thankfully, even in my grief-stricken state, I was able to recognize the inherent weirdness of cryogenically preserving my mother's bean salad.

We divvied up the responsibilities for the memorial service the next day. Dad's decades as a bureaucrat made him the logical choice to take point as overall project manager; Kirk, with his background in corporate communications, certainly had the core competencies to handle the service's program design; Paul's experience as a chef made him the natural choice for catering; and I would finally get a chance to put the tens-of-thousands of dollars thrown away on film school to good use as the audio-visual guy for my mother's funeral.

As Audio-Visual Coordinator, I had two main items on my list—document the ceremony (I would be shooting video and stills) and prepare the memorial photo album.

Piece of cake.

Or so I thought until confronted with THE BOX. The box of a thousand snapshots, little scraps of my mother's life, most yellowed and curling under just as her toes had been right before her body was reduced to ash. Handling these pictures, the corpus of her dead memories, made me squeamish. I stayed up all night before the memorial, digging deep into the box searching for the images that would put her life into some sort of coherent perspective.

Most pictures are actually not worth a thousand words. The only pictures we think to take are the obvious ones, the routine photo-ops of birthdays and weddings; the ribbon-cuttings of life. But the key moments of our lives most often start off as the cast-off variety. It's only when looking in the rearview mirror that we can see which turns in the road took us to where we are today. Which routine kiss good-bye would be *the* kiss good-bye. Which argument-ending "last words" would be *the* last words. There are no high-definition images of these most defining moments of our lives. Just the smudge of memory.

I wish I had a picture of my mother from the evening after she made that scene at the restaurant. That would be worth much more than a thousand words to me. Mom making a scene had taken care of ruining the evening on the early side, leaving our family with a rare couple hours of daylight to enjoy each other's company without having to worry about when something bad was going to happen. It was finally pleasant outside, a cool breeze. Paul found an old Frisbee somewhere, and he and Kirk started tossing it back and forth in the front yard.

I watched them from the front steps, feeling the breeze on my face. Mom sat down next to me.

"I'm sorry, honey," she said.

"Sorry for what?" I said, not really listening to her.

"Tonight at the restaurant and . . . and all the other times. You shouldn't have had to take care of me in order to get the love you needed."

This was my mom, too—these rare moments of utter clarity, complete selflessness, and love in which she said things you'd been waiting your entire life to hear. I was speechless.

"Honey, did you hear me?"

"Yeah."

I wiped my eyes and looked at Sam and my niece Casey running in the yard, Kirk and Paul sharing a joke as they whipped the Frisbee back and forth, Dad setting out lawn chairs: simple, normal, family moments.

"Your eyes look so sad, honey. What's the matter?" Mom said.

"I just wish . . . I don't know . . . "

"I understand, honey."

And she did, she really did. For the first time in such a long time she'd really been my mother that night, rubbing my back, making everything all right.

I got up and we ran around in the street tossing the Frisbee back and forth. It was the magic hour, that hour of perfect, rose-colored light just before dusk. In the dying light of that day, all of us were beautiful: Kirk's showboating and competitiveness now just Kirk being Kirk; Paul's awkwardness somehow adorable; Dad still spry, running around like a kid despite his seventy-odd years; and Mom just smiling, drinking it all in, as close to happy as I ever remember seeing her.

Why was it that these happy moments, when they happened at all, always seemed to come at the end of our family visits, as the parting gift, the set of steak knives? What I find most haunting about my family is not all the difficult dinners, not the painful silences, but, instead, these Frisbee games, these moments of accidental loveliness in which we glimpsed the happiness that might have been.

I deeply regret all the years I wasted in anger, hating my mother for not being the mom I wanted her to be. I wanted the one all the Hallmark cards were written for: the milk-and-cookies-waiting-for-you-after-school mom, the kiss-and-make-it-all-better-world's-greatest mom. It was only after my mother was gone that it even occurred to me to wonder if *I* was the son she wanted *me* to be.

It is the image of my mother on that Frisbee night, in that perfect, painful, magic-hour light, that the passing of time has fixed in the photo album of my heart as the one to remember her by. She seemed at peace that night. I'd like to believe that she found her peace, even if just for five minutes one summer evening before the sun went down. Mom believed in reincarnation, so, who knows, maybe she'll be luckier the next time around.

I'd like to believe that, too.

Chapter Eleven

CUMBERLAND GAP

DANIEL BOONE COUNTRY. That's where we were. Dad and I came off the Natchez Trace Parkway near Memphis and stopped for dinner at a truck stop before heading north through the Cumberland Gap. Part of Daniel Boone's legend was how he and a team of thirty-five axmen blazed a trail through the Cumberland Gap, gateway to the west. In their honor, I ordered the Lumberjack breakfast for dinner while Dad went for the heart-healthy soup-and-salad combo. We each ordered an extra-large coffee. We had miles to go before we slept that night if we wanted to make New York by the next day.

As Dad hit the boys' room, I studied a picture that Rose had texted me on my cell phone, a missive from behind the iron curtain of "not talking" Rose had imposed for slights as real to her as they were imagined to me. The picture was a family portrait of the three of them lying in bed. The boys were freshly pajama'd, hair still wet from bath time. Benny lay on his back, his kicking legs a blur, face aglow with that Benny smile that lights the world. Sam had snuck his angel face into the frame as he took the picture the way he's seen me do. I couldn't help but look for the scar on his nose from the dog bite. You almost couldn't see it. Almost. I made myself look at his smile instead.

And there, smack-dab in the middle of all this happy was Rose, looking like the end of the world; a thousand-yard stare right through the camera.

We hadn't talked since Vicksburg, that argument in the Applebee's. What had it been about anyway? I scratched my head. Hard to recall even though it happened just the day before yesterday. All our arguments lately seemed to be about everything and nothing at the same time, making it hard to tell one from another.

I finally remembered. Air conditioning. The argument in Vicksburg had been about air conditioning. When did we become these people? We argued about everything. *Everything.* Even my mother's death.

I had been down in Virginia for three days with my brothers and my dad. During that time we had made arrangements for Mom to be cremated, spread her ashes, done a little bit of planning for the memorial service, and drank a lot of beer.

Rose was losing patience.

"If this was Jewish, the funeral would've been three days ago and the whole thing would've been catered," Rose said on the phone.

"Okay, well . . . it's a little late to convert, but I'll make a note of that for the next time my mother dies," I said.

Getting to say whatever the hell you want is one of the few perks of grief.

"Honey, I was joking."

"Sorry, I'm not really in a joking mood. My mother just died."

"I'm worried about you."

"I'm fine."

"You don't sound fine."

"Well, my mother just died."

"She died three days ago."

"Well, that still makes her dead as far as I know."

"Honey, you don't sound good."

"Well . . . my mother died."

"You keep saying that."

"It's kind of a big deal, take my word for it."

"Honey, don't be that way, I'm just trying to—"

"I know, I know . . . look, I've got to go."

"Wait! When are we coming down?"

"I don't know yet. We're still figuring out the memorial service, when people can come in and everything."

"Don't you want me there?"

"Rose, please—"

"You shouldn't be down there by yourself, it's not healthy."

"I'm not alone, I'm with my family."

"What about me? The kids? We're not family?"

"Honey, of course you and the kids are my family."

"Then we should be there with you. I should be at your side. It's what a wife does."

"In your family's tradition."

"I thought we were your family."

"My . . . *family of origin*, okay?" I really resented her for making me say things like *family of origin* at a time like this. "I'm really sorry that my *family of origin* isn't Jewish and we don't have the benefit of a five-thousand-year-old cultural tradition to tell us where to stand and when to cry and what caterer to call, okay? We're winging it here!" I yelled before hanging up.

I actually envied Rose her list of thou-shalts, her certainty about every family member's place in times of trial, even her firm belief in the transformative power of catering. But my family of origin had always been a much more ad hoc, come-as-you-are affair.

"CAN I ASK YOU A QUESTION?" I asked Dad as I poured pancake syrup onto my Lumberjack after the waitress brought us our food. "What did you and Mom argue about?"

"We argued about . . . ah . . . let's see, ah . . . " Dad chuckled. "You know, I really don't remember . . . "

"You don't remember arguing with Mom? *I* remember."

"But we saw most things the same way—finances, politics, all that sort of business. We didn't have differences of opinion—we were just . . . very different people."

"Well, I wouldn't argue with you there," I said. We chuckled.

"What do you and Rose argue about?"

"Oh, you know . . . the designated hitter mainly."

"Is that right?"

"Nonstop. Rose is National League all the way, sees the DH as sacrilege, whereas my question is, who is *she* to tell Big Papi he can't play baseball."

"Big Papi?"

"He's the DH for the Boston Red Sox."

"You're ducking the question."

"Nothing gets past you," I said, joking.

"You tell jokes as a defense mechanism."

"*Defense mechanism*—that's a big word for you, Dad."

"I learned it from your mother. I just *pretended* not to listen to her."

We laughed.

"It's okay," Dad said. "We don't have to talk about it."

He sipped his coffee while I studied his magnificent old-man eyebrows. They had a life of their own. At the moment, one was turned up, the other down, like the masks for comedy and tragedy. His eyes looked tired from a long day on the road. All his endless days at the office had worn permanent circles under his eyes. He was seventy-five now. He had licked the cancer and was so active that it was hard to think of him as old, but seventy-five wasn't exactly young, either.

There would be plenty of time for us to "not talk about things" after he was gone.

"Actually, I . . . I do want to talk about it," I said. "The hardest thing for me is . . . is to have gone through all the things that Rose and I went through, survive all that, win that war, and now be at such different places . . . losing the peace, I guess you could say. Hard times are supposed to pull a family together. It's funny, I . . . I actually miss it sometimes."

"Miss what?"

"The hard times. I liked knowing what I was supposed to do. I mean, having Benny at death's door was *hard,* but it wasn't *complicated.* All I could do was be there for him. Let him hear my voice. Hold his hand. And I did that. I didn't sleep for four days, until it looked like he started to pull through. But now . . . now things are . . . complicated. I just don't know how to help Rose."

"What does she need help with?"

"What *doesn't* she need help with? She's worrying herself to death . . . she can't sleep, can't eat . . . gets ulcers, migraines, asthma attacks, anxiety attacks . . . anxiety attacks about whether or not she's having an asthma attack—she has a gift for unhappiness, I'm telling you."

"Have you talked to her about seeing a doctor?"

"Dad, that's about *all* I talk to her about. But if I push too hard, she says, you know, if she's such a burden, why don't I just leave her? It's a real conversation killer, I'm telling you."

Dad smiled. I could tell it took effort. "She just needs a chance to get back on her feet again. She'll be fine," he said, patting me on the shoulder.

I wondered if he really believed that, or if "fine" was just his version of a conversation killer, profoundly nicer than Rose's but no less effective.

Dad excused himself to make another pit stop in the men's room before we got back on the road, and I looked again at the picture on the cell phone, not wanting to recognize how much of my mother I could see in Rose and how much of my younger self I could see in Sam, still happy, not wised up yet to all the unhappiness around him. When you're six years old, everything in the world is a toy or a game until proven otherwise.

Even depressed mothers.

"HERE'S YOUR WATER, Mrs. Millhone. Take your pill," Sam said to Rose, speaking in his low, pretend-doctor's voice as they played a game of Rose and Dr. Sam—their version of Joe and Mr. Peacock.

"Yes, doctor," Rose said, smiling as Sam took her pulse. Rose comes from a family of doctors, so she was delighted by Sam demonstrating an early interest in taking care of the afflicted. Coming from the family that I came from, all I could see was how I'd been afflicted by being my mother's caretaker. Watching them play doctor this way sent chills up my spine.

"May I have a word with the patient?" I said, cutting in.

"Okay, but then she needs to rest," Sam said, exiting to continue his rounds.

"I don't think him pretending to take care of you when you're not feeling well is a healthy game."

"But he likes to make me feel better. It makes him happy."

"It makes him *responsible*. If he feels like he's the one who makes you feel better, how do you think he'll feel when he *can't*? It'll fuck him up. I do not want our son fucked up."

"Mark, I'm not your mother."

"Then stop acting like her."

"Get out of here!" Rose said, beyond offended.

Unfortunately, certain words cannot go unsaid. Or certain thoughts, un-thunk. Forming a mental association between your wife and your dead mother does not do wonders for your libido. I couldn't remember the last time we'd touched, could barely recognize her as the same vibrant woman I had fallen in love with a lifetime ago. She had the most dazzling freckles that summer. I missed kissing them. She left her room so rarely now that her freckles had all but abandoned her and taken my kisses with them.

"WHAT WAS IT LIKE when you and Mom first got together?" I asked Dad after we got back on the road, our backs to a beautiful sunset as we headed east through the Cumberland Gap. After we cleared that, the road would turn north again. We wanted to put a healthy chunk of Virginia behind us before stopping for the night.

Dad shook his head, a silly, lopsided grin dancing around the edges of his mouth.

"It was just . . . it was . . . "

"Yeah?"

"*Rapture,*" Dad finally said.

You could have given a monkey a Rubik's Cube and he would have solved it long before I would have guessed that the next word out of my Dad's mouth was going to be "rapture," especially in relation to my mother.

"God, she was a beautiful woman," he went on. "Just so . . . ripe. We made love on our first date. She had this basement apartment. We didn't know that people could see in the windows—"

"Okay, um, thanks for the over-share, Dad," I said, holding up my hand to make him stop. I wasn't sure exactly how I wanted to remember my mother, but I was pretty sure it wasn't as something out of *Penthouse Forum.*

"You were really happy together at the beginning, weren't you?"

"Well, of course we were. Why else do you get married?"

"Of course," I said, shaking my head.

Even more haunting to me than the bitter, burnt-out people that I knew as my parents growing up was the thought that once upon a time they too had been happy—just like Rose and me, just like every other couple that says "I do." Happiness is either an accident or a gift, never a guarantee.

"You got married really fast, didn't you? Was it because of the war? I always wondered about that." My father was drafted near the end of the Korean War and spent his service at Fort Bliss, Texas, training radar operators and never saw combat.

"Well, when we met, I was 1A for Korea, so I knew the letter could come any day, but really we just loved each other and we both came from families that were less than happy and we were eager to start our own."

"That's really, ah . . . funny," I said, not laughing. I'd married Rose to get out of an unhappy family formed by the union of two people who got married to get out of *their* unhappy families. And so on and so on. Probably goes all the way back to the begats in the Bible.

I opened my cell phone once more, thinking to call Rose to say goodnight, to say . . . what? Something that would change things somehow, but what? Who was she anymore? I wasn't sure. Where had my soul mate gone? I knew Rose was asking herself the same thing about me. On the occasion of our last anniversary, she had written me a loving, heartfelt e-mail to inform me that I was no longer the man she married:

I was hoping that we would be able to talk tonight after watch-ing our wedding video, that seeing who we were then would inspire conversation. Since that was not possible, I still have to get what is going on inside me out. I can't go to sleep with all of these emotions filling my brain and my heart.

The most difficult thing for me about watching that video was not recognizing the people we were. Who we are right now, at least to me, bears no resemblance to who those people were. People who believed in each other and were desperate to be together, could not keep their eyes or hands off each other, and clearly behaved as though they were two halves of a whole, not the two completely separate entities we function as now. I can't remember the last time we felt anything close to that kind of passion, and I am not talking physical, I am talking emotional.

I am not sure when exactly the pivotal moment it started slipping was, or even if there was one; maybe we are just two people growing apart and have to make a very important choice of whether we come back together and rediscover those people in that video or we go our separate ways and follow our individual quests. I can't continue this limbo, waiting for things to return to normal yet seeing no sign that they ever will . . . it is too lonely and it is too sad.

The person I married was my soul mate. He was my dreams realized and heaven brought to me. Are you that person still? If so, where are you? That goofy, silly, light-hearted, intense with passion not with anger, romantic, tearful, gentle man who accepted me and all my quirks. Who laughed at me in a way that made me laugh too, not cry. Who made me feel that love was all that mattered. That life was "permanent" and if nothing ever happens but our love, it would still be a perfect life. You are now even literally colorless. This intense figure in black. This dark and angry shadow that scares me. Who are you?

Watching that video, seeing how happy we once were, how madly in love with you I was, just shattered me. I mourn for that couple. Watching that video, you would really think if any couple would make it, it would be them. Now, I am not sure what the ending of our story will be. I went into this marriage trusting every vow, not even close to a question in my mind that we would be together forever, that our love would age like fine wine and get better and bolder and richer with each year. How did we come to a place where we are space partners in a bed and that is all? Where did we go? I want to be with someone who loves me like the man in that video, not that tolerates me like the man that I live with.

I want the man in the video to come back. The "life is permanent" man, that values love and happiness above all. That man is the partner I need, the person that inspires me and makes me feel safe. He believed in me despite all of my flaws, he loved me for who I was. I remember, he would tell me that all the time. I don't know how to begin to find him again, or if you still even want him to exist. I don't even know when we can talk about it, as we can't talk in front of Sam, and you are tired and asleep almost immediately after he's tucked in his bed.

I don't want this marriage to end, but I also just cannot be a good parent if I am an unhappy, scared person. So I am lost.

I want to hear what you feel, but I don't know when or

*how, because of your schedule, you will have to be in touch
with me.*

—Wife

You will have to be in touch with me . . .

As Dad and I drove on into deepening dusk, the shadowed shoulders of the great Cumberland Gap rising up on either side of us, I
turned that expression over in my mind. How was it possible that
the gap between Rose and me had grown so great that words as
impersonal, as perfunctory, as "you will have to be in touch with
me" had become our mode of address on the occasion of our anniversary?

I was losing her—not to another suitor, but simply to the past, to
bad luck, to all that had befallen us, to the shit in "shit happens."

"You okay? Need a break?" Dad asked.

To which I, of course, replied—

"No. I'm fine."

Chapter Twelve

SALTVILLE

WE CROSSED OVER the Virginia border and into the foothills of the Blue Ridge Mountains. I couldn't see them, not even their shadows, in the full black night. Only the Bomber's engine, working almost imperceptibly harder, told me the mountains had begun. We passed a sign for Saltville and yet another historical marker for yet another battle of the Civil War. After a while, you begin to wonder if it wouldn't be easier—and less depressing— to mark the spots where people didn't die. I never did get the whole Civil War reenactment thing. I don't need to run around some farmer's field on a hot summer day wearing wool pants and uncomfortable old shoes just for the privilege of pretending to die. My own life has afforded me abundant painful experiences that I can, and often do, relive in the comfort of my own home.

Were I forced to choose a Civil War battle to reenact, I would favor the more discreet charms of the Battle of Saltville over the hoary gore fests of Gettysburg or Antietam. The saltworks at Saltville were the last under Confederate control, and had the Civil War not ended with a bang at Appomattox a few months later, the Union's conquest of little old Saltville could very well have decided the outcome of the war. Without salt to preserve their food, the Confederacy would have slowly starved to death.

It's the little things, as common as salt, that will get you in the end.

"I should have called the boys to say goodnight, but now it's too late," I said to Dad, his face glowing softly in the lights from the dash.

"Bet you'll get quite the homecoming when you get back," he said.

"*Quite* the homecoming," I cracked. "Maybe from the boys, but I don't really see Rose hanging any 'Welcome Home' banners in my honor."

We actually used to do that, put up banners to welcome Rose or me back from business trips. But one day we just stopped being those people. It happened that Easter of the big snow when Rose came back from Australia, her first business trip after Benny was born. Thankfully, her plane got in before the sky opened up and the freak March blizzard shut down the city.

From New York, "down under" is about as far away as far away gets. Funny, the sixteen-hour time difference got Rose and me more in sync than we'd been in months. All the stress of Benny's time in the hospital, my mother passing away, etc., had widened our natural circadian-rhythm divide (Rose is a night owl while I have farm-boy genes) to the point that Rose usually fell asleep about the time I woke up. In our scratchy phone connections during her sojourn down under, we pledged to have fun again, to work to rekindle the mighty whimsy that was the magic of us. Rose's return, on that snowy Easter Sunday, was on March 27th, which also happened to be the anniversary of our first kiss.

What better day to make the first day of the rest of your lives?

In the spirit of these proceedings, I told Sam to go heavy on the glitter for Rose's "Welcome Home" banner. I rolled out a long piece of brown contractor paper on the floor, and we all went at it. After Sam filled in my big block letters with the glitter, he unleashed his inner Jackson Pollock, wanging artful paint spatters everywhere. Benny, then just nine months old, giggled and cooed as I pressed his soft baby hands into the cool glop of the paint to make bright handprints on the dark brown paper. This, apparently, inspired Boomer; he stepped into the paint and decorated the banner—not to mention the rest of our apartment—with his rainbow paw prints.

It felt good.

Cheesy-movie-dance-around-in-your-pj's-to-Motown good.

"That is *the* most beautiful thing I've ever seen," Rose said when she got home and saw our banner, a glittering, paint-splattered mess that only a mother could love—but since it was all for her, that's all that mattered. Rose broke out an entire duty-free gift shop's worth of priceless junk, all manner of down-under souvenirs, including a stuffed koala bear that said "G'day Mate!" when you pulled the string on its neck and a "never-fail genuine Aussie boomerang" that I seemed genuinely unable to make boomerang back to me.

The snow started to fall in the early afternoon and was expected to last all night. The prospect of getting snowed in felt almost impossibly cozy; a home is never warmer than when it's cold outside. When it finally came time to put Benny to bed, I did the honors in the nursery while Rose, jet-lagged, curled up on our bed with Boomer at her feet.

"Mommy needs cuddles!" Rose called out to Sam, still playing with his haul of priceless junk out in the living room.

"Sam, you get your little tushie in this bed *this instant,*" she added playfully as Sam taxied his die-cast metal Qantas airliner across the living room rug. Sam smiled and then, making jet engine sounds by whistling through his perfect niblet teeth, took off with the airliner, bound for bedtime and mommy cuddles. As I gave Benny his go-to-sleep bottle in the nursery, I heard Sam's stocking feet pitter-pattering the length of the living room, and then he made a flying, cruising-altitude leap up onto our bed in the master bedroom.

And then I heard the cry.

That keening shriek of shock and pain that cuts through everything. All children make this same sound when injured, and yet, even in the after-school din of a crowded playground, when it's your child, you just know.

"Mark, I need you!" Rose called out from our bedroom as I carefully pulled Benny's bottle from his sleep-slack lips.

"Oh my god, *Mark!*" Rose called again.

"Shhhhh . . . " I breathed as Benny drowsily fussed—whatever just happened, it couldn't be worth waking the baby.

"What happened?" I asked, finally emerging from the nursery, closing the door behind me, cat-burglar quiet. Rose stood in the kitchen with Sam, her face as pale as the wad of white Kleenex she had pressed to Sam's nose. It took a moment to register that the red spattered on Sam's baseball shirt and dripping onto the floor was not from our "Welcome Home Mommy" painting party earlier that day.

It was blood.

"What . . . what happened?" I stuttered.

"Boomer!" Sam choked out, betrayed.

There is a reason you let sleeping dogs lie. When Sam had sailed onto our bed with his toy jet plane, he landed right on Boomer, asleep at Rose's feet. Boomer, startled awake from his dog dream, snapped at whatever had attacked him. He got Sam right between the eyes.

Sam couldn't see his wound, and Rose couldn't bear to look at it, so they both stared at me to see how bad it was. I did my best to keep a poker face as I pulled aside the wad of bloody Kleenex to reveal a jagged, bone-deep, two-inch rip down the center of Sam's nose.

"Call 911," I said, and then, looking at the desperate-afraid faces of Rose and Sam, I lied to them, "It's ah . . . it's just a scratch, really. But we should take him to the emergency room now, just in case."

"Emergency room?" Rose asked. She took one look at the gash and promptly called an ambulance.

"Boomer! Why'd you do that?!" Sam yelled in shock and anger.

I spied the dog cowering under the bed and went for him. A ribbon of pee laced the floor as I hauled Boomer out by the collar, lifting all of his eighty pounds like nothing and throwing him into the bathroom as if I were tossing a bag of garbage to the curb. As I slammed the door behind me, I heard Rose yell, "Mark, stop! You'll kill him!"

She was right to worry. I had killed our other dog, hadn't I? Put Bailey down because I thought I must to keep our children safe?

And now it was my old friend Boomer, the dog I spared, who had betrayed me, mauled my sweet boy. I was wearing heavy boots that day, and I tell you Boomer knew it. I kicked him in the ribs, the haunch, the head. He yelped as if the sound had been ripped from his body as he skittered back into the corner, cowering behind the toilet. Some dark, wounded animal place in me did the instant math—if I stomped on Boomer's head with my heavy boots, I could kill him. Kill him dead for what he did to Sam. It would be easy. And by some ancient blood calculus, fair.

"Daddy!" I heard Sam yell through the bathroom door.

Sam's voice brought me back to myself, back to my family and back to the truth of the matter—this bite, ultimately, was my fault, not Boomer's. It would never have happened if I had trained the dog off the bed as I shoulda-woulda-coulda done. As I stood there, breathing heavy, my foot hurting from kicking the dog, I looked down into Boomer's terrified dumb animal eyes and wondered: What had I done with the five minutes a day it would have taken to prevent my son from being maimed?

THE PLASTIC SURGEON was a reassuringly handsome man.

I watched from a chair next to Sam's bed in the emergency room at St. Vincent's Hospital as the surgeon used his large, canny hands to stick a needle into Sam's face. A syringe of some painkiller. The doctor mosquitoed all around the wound with his needle, pricking it numb, and then, using forceps, threaded the curved suture needle he would use to stitch up Sam.

I looked on, feeling oddly nostalgic for the first time I saw Sam bleed. At his bris, the sight of Sam's blood when the mohel performed the circumcision made me faint. Rose's uncles had to sit me down in the chair reserved for Elijah. But there had been so many doctors since then. I could now look on with near-academic detachment as the surgeon pierced Sam's torn flesh with the curved fishhook of the suture needle. He stitched for what seemed like hours.

"Will Sam have a scar?" I finally worked up the nerve to ask.

I braced for his answer, grateful that his words would be for me alone. Rose was home with Benny, and poor Sam had fallen asleep while getting stitches, so spent was he from his ordeal—not just the bite, but the ambulance ride through whiteout blizzard streets only to wait and wait some more for this plastic surgeon, apparently the one Jewish doctor not celebrating Easter. I found it instructive that, before answering the question of whether Sam would have a scar, the doctor studied my face, not Sam's—gauging his answer more on what he thought I could handle than what he had to say.

"Well," he said finally. "It's a very deep cut, very jagged. A lot will depend on him, on how he heals."

I hated this answer, essentially the same one we got when we asked about Benny's prognosis in Intensive Care. Why should such ultimate burdens fall upon their tiny shoulders?

"There must be *something* we can do," I said, holding Sam's pliant hand in mine, so soft, so vulnerable.

"What I can guarantee you is that no matter how well this heals, for a long time, when you look at his face, you'll see nothing else but the scar. I'm saying that as a father, not a surgeon. Our daughter got bit in the face by our cocker spaniel. Very common at this age, the kid's face is right at the dog's level, you know? Was it a big dog?"

I nodded. "Eighty pounds."

"Wow. You were lucky. It could've been *much* worse."

It was the right thing for him to say, but to actually consider this—to postulate what might have happened had the bite come half an inch to the left or to the right, to visualize Sam losing an eye—did not comfort me.

Having spent so much time with doctors during our family's year from hell had a curious effect on me. The better their bedside manner, the less I liked having them around. The more practiced the bedside manner, the more it made me wonder how many situations just like ours the doctor had handled, made me think of how commonplace misery was, the norm of life and not the exception.

Four seemed an unfair age to make Sam learn that life wasn't fair.

When we finally walked out of the emergency room, it was past midnight. A white gauze bandage covered the mess of stitches running down the center of Sam's nose. Outside St. Vincent's, the snow had continued to fall, rendering the city inappropriately postcard-lovely. I carried Sam through the drifts until I finally succeeded in hailing a cab.

We got in and I hugged Sam, smelling both the bitter funk of all his hours sweating out this ordeal and the cold, alcohol clean of the hospital. We were riding the way we always do in a cab, him on my lap with the seat belt over both of us like we're one person. It's like that somehow with fathers and sons.

I retrieved a voice mail from my dad after we got into the cab:

"Mark, it's your dad. Got . . . got Rose's message about Sam . . . that's just . . . just . . . I really want to be there for you. The blizzard's just got everything between Washington and New York pretty well shut down. Flights are grounded out of National. Interstate's blocked. Only thing running is the trains. I called Amtrak and with the holiday and the storm, everything's sold out, so I, ah . . . ah . . . "

I hung up. Dad not being there when I really needed him was as routine as bad weather, but I just couldn't take one more thing that day. Not that day. I knew I was being unfair, that Dad really wanted to be there, but still, I wished Rose hadn't called him, hadn't gotten my hopes up.

Calling in Dad for reinforcement was just part of the shock-and-awe campaign Rose waged to take Sam's mind off the dog bite. Some people turn to the Good Book in times of trouble. Rose takes comfort in "to do" lists. By the time I got home from the hospital and we tucked Sam into bed that night, she'd already mobilized friends and family, planned a toy-shopping sortie to FAO Schwarz, requisitioned a signed baseball from Sam's favorite major-league baseball player, and consulted a preeminent child psychologist on the best way to handle the situation for Sam.

"He said to do it quickly. By tomorrow, if we can," Rose said.

"Do what?" I asked, trying not to hear Boomer whining in the bathroom where he'd been confined since the bite happened.

"Get the new dog."

"*The new dog?*"

"The therapist said giving Sam the opportunity to select a new dog would be the most empowering, therapeutic way to help him move on, not be afraid of dogs—"

"Just slow down," I cut in. "I haven't figured out how to deal with the old one yet."

"Well, we have to get rid of him," Rose said.

"I know he . . . can't stay here but . . . *get rid of him?*" I groaned.

"Maybe there's a farm somewhere—"

"There are no farms, okay? I've been through this. Definitely not for a dog that bites a kid."

Boomer, as if following our conversation from the bathroom, yelped pitifully.

"But it wasn't really Boomer's fault," Rose said.

I turned away from her, shook my head.

"What?"

"Maybe there's a farm for *me* somewhere," I finally said.

"Honey. It's not your fault. I'm the one who told Sam to jump up on the bed with me. I was just so tired from the trip."

I shook my head as I thought about how epic this day had been for her, starting off half a world away, down under. She was so jet-lagged that her body thought it was yesterday. If only it were. If only we could take back the actual blood, sweat, and tears of this day. The anniversary of our first kiss. The happy "Welcome Home Mommy!" banner we'd painted that morning still hung on the wall, but when I looked at Sam's artful paint spatters, all I could think about was his blood dripping on the floor.

"The dogs were always my responsibility," I said.

"But *I* made Sam jump up on the bed and then Boomer—"

She flinched as if seeing the dog bite for the first time.

Boomer yelped louder.

"Make him stop!" Rose said with such anguish I wondered if she meant Boomer's yelping or the bite itself, now playing in a 3-D Technicolor loop inside her head.

"Boomer, hush!" I yelled.

Silence reigned for one blissful moment and then . . .

Benny started to cry.

"I just got him down after the last feeding!" Rose wailed. "I'm sorry . . . I . . . I can't deal with this right now!" She shook her head as she retreated to our bedroom, still her sanctuary despite the fact that the dog bite had officially rendered it the most dangerous room in the house.

"Daddy? Daddy, I need you!" Sam called from his room.

Rose's door slammed, the baby cried, the dog yelped, Sam called my name, and then, just when I thought I was feeling overwhelmed, the phone rang.

It rang a number of times before I realized it must be for me; that this strange, unhappy place filled with weeping and wailing was, in fact, my house. I've never felt more alone than at that moment, surrounded by my family's unhappiness. We'd suffered mightily over the past year, but this was the first time we'd been truly unhappy. Up until then, we'd been crimeless victims—my father's cancer, Benny's illness, and my mother's passing had all been acts of God, mere chance. But in Sam's wound was the salt of our guilt. With it would come recriminations, blame, a wedge between Rose and me quickly filled by all our displaced anger over all the things that had happened to our family—injuries not so easily stitched.

"Are you going to get that?!" Rose called from our bedroom.

"Hello?" I finally said, diving for the phone.

"Mark, it's your dad. How are you doing?"

"Well . . . I've been better. You?"

"Fine. Look, Amtrak said on the phone everything was sold out—"

"I know, Dad, it's okay, don't worry about it."

"Well, I figured the thing to do was just to go down to the station and try to get on a train anyway. I finally got on one and it looks like I'll have to stand all the way to New York, but I'll get there. You just hang on, son. I'll be there. I love you."

The events of that day and of the whole year from hell leading up to it had steeled me against everything—everything except unexpected acts of kindness.

I wept.

Chapter Thirteen

THE SCHOOL
FOR BOYS

DAD'S TRAIN ARRIVED in New York late that night, in the wee hours of Monday, after that Easter Sunday of snow and blood. After I picked him up, we drove north, out of the city, taking Boomer upstate to the Mohawk and Hudson River Humane Society. I still had half a box of the Purina T-Bonz brand dog biscuits left over from Bailey's last supper. Boomer liked them just as much as she did.

After we got to the humane society, I doled out the biscuits one by one, trying to make the box last forever. The five minutes I told Cydney I needed to say good-bye to Boomer stretched on and on, biscuit after biscuit, for more than an hour. My knees went numb kneeling next to him there on the gravel dog run. I patted his back, broader than the span of my hand. It had been this strong back that had borne Sam on countless horsey rides, this shoulder I'd leaned on during my trip down to Virginia to watch my mother die. He was such a comfort then, always at my side; the warm, uncomplicated bulk of him like a ballast keeping me upright.

"So, there's no one who can take him?" I asked Cydney, looking on from the other side of the dog run's chain-link fence. She shook her head slowly, infinitely tired and infinitely patient. She bore the responsibility for the life and death of all the animals under her watch as matter-of-factly as she wore her stained overalls and rubber boots—life and death's a messy business, a girl's gotta dress for it.

"If I didn't have seven dogs at my house already, I'd take him in myself, but . . . " She trailed off, or maybe I just couldn't hear her over the dull roar of what was not being said.

There is no farm.

All I'd ever really wanted was a dog, that's what I told Rose once. The occasion was the first of my birthdays that we celebrated as a couple. She took me to a fancy restaurant, the kind of place where you have to know what all the silverware is for, and I just sat there, rearranging my peas. The place was lost on me. I just wanted to be home. Wherever that was. After all my grad school years with little more than my ambition to keep me company in the big city, I was homesick for a place I'd never really lived, a family I'd never really had. If only I could have a dog, then I would be home, I told Rose that birthday night. What is a dog, really, but an idea of home? An intimation of the hearth, a vision of one's very feet as worthy to curl up before?

All the dogs of my childhood had been ill-fated. First there was Cloud, the puffy purebred Samoyed, who just up and disappeared one fine Christmas Eve in Des Moines. Then a mutt fatefully named Axle who did not survive collision with same. And finally Myrtle, a pound puppy I named after a nice lady on my paper route but my brother Kirk retrained to answer to Butt-face. Butt-face couldn't make the move with our family to Virginia because, according to my father, the apartment buildings there just didn't take dogs.

Bailey and Boomer were my second chance, not just to have a dog, but to feel like I was home. For this reason, the dog bite went much deeper than the clash of tooth and flesh; it went to the very heart of us. If Boomer was wrong, then every other thing that had been part of that great whimsy that threw Rose and me together was now suspect. Rose had stood up at our wedding and told everyone that I was her luck. Oh, we had lots of luck—it's just that most of it was bad.

Boomer took the final biscuit.

He snouted around for more, pressing his wet nose into my hand, and I said, "Sorry, old pal. I'm empty. You took everything."

Cydney waited for me to give her the nod. The veterinary technician waited inside the humane society building to give Boomer the shot. Dad waited in the car. All waiting for me to be the man here, to do what needed to be done.

Well, they were all going to have to wait a little bit longer.

I just felt too guilty. I hugged Boomer and listened to the barking of all the other dogs from all the other broken homes. Dogs don't end up at the humane society because they cease to be dogs, but because someone's cherished notion of their home as a place large enough, stable enough, loving enough to care for a pet got reduced to bricks and mortar, a mere house. The dogs, inconveniently, live on after someone's idea of home has died.

What the hell was I going to do with Boomer?

IT TURNS OUT there is a farm—you just have to pay for it.

Cydney found a farmer who agreed, for a fee, to board Boomer until I either located him a home or got the nerve to put him down. Like most answers to impossible questions, it didn't really answer anything. It seemed oddly fitting to me that the farmer's price for assuaging or, at least, postponing my guilt was roughly the same as my minimum monthly balance for a credit card on which I'd done some serious damage. Guilt is like credit card debt—it kills you, but try living without it. Once you suck up the stiff premium of believing you had the power to prevent a horrible accident that occurred in the past, you get to roll over that illusion of control and apply it to any horrible accidents that may occur in the future. Or, put another way: The horrible accident didn't just happen. You *made* it happen. This means you have the power to make it *not* happen again.

After leaving Boomer at the farm, Dad and I drove in silence for several minutes before realizing we had no idea where we were going. Everything looked familiar. And strange. Like the farm stand we passed advertising "Homemade Produce, Fresh Fudge." The winding country road we were on had to go somewhere— someone had bothered to pave it, after all—but all our best efforts to make sure we weren't just going in circles took us right past that same odd farm stand once again.

"Let's just head south," Dad said, yawning.

"Is that the direction back to the highway?"

"That's the direction back to New York City."

"Dad, it's two hundred miles."

He shrugged. "We'll get there eventually. At least we'll know we're getting lost in the right direction."

The nice thing about getting lost—which is hard to enjoy while you're actually lost—is that you're forced to take note of your surroundings. The land becomes a live thing, a mystery in which you need to find yourself. Every turn of the road opens up a new chapter, a new set of landmarks that might take you home. That line of trees there . . . didn't I see that before? This curve in the road, doesn't it feel familiar? The place you are lost somehow always feels the same. I imagine that whenever I get lost, I always go to some Brigadoon with a Native American name that opens up whenever I go off the map—WHEREDAFUCKAMI or WHYDIDN'TIMAP QUESTIT.

"Mohonk–Cragsmoor," Dad read off the first sign we passed in what seemed like forever. Time moves more slowly in the land of the lost. "I'll be darned, must be close to that school Paul went to," Dad continued, shaking his head.

My oldest brother, Paul was, from the start, a child both challenged and challenging. Born seven weeks premature in a time when preemies were not expected to live, he refused to die. Didn't speak until he was two years old but then spoke in complete sentences. Resisted my father's efforts to teach him chess but then quickly became unbeatable. After Paul spent most of the second grade just staring into space, my parents had him evaluated by a child psychologist, who recommended the Mohonk-Cragsmoor School for Boys as the kind of place where Paul could get the kind of highly structured learning environment he needed to fulfill his potential. The school was very expensive, so my parents could only afford to send him there for a single year.

"How old was Paul when he went away to that school?" I asked.

"Ah . . . it was third grade . . . "

"That would make him eight . . . young to be away from home," I said.

"The day we dropped him off, I . . . I remember looking back in the rearview mirror. Paul chased the car as far as he could, yelling for me to stop . . . " Dad trailed off, shaking his head. "It was what they said he needed, you know, the experts, but it was a mistake, I see that now. You shouldn't be away from your family when you're that young. It's so clear to me now, but at the time I . . . I just didn't know what to do."

In that one moment, I understood my father as never before. When you're a kid, you tend to assume that your parents actually know what they're doing. They had to get a license to drive a car, so they must have one for all the other stuff parents do, right? But my dad was just making up the whole father thing as he went along, praying there would be no pop quizzes to catch him with his pants down. The guy was faking it the whole time. But so was I. I had no clue how to handle the ongoing catastrophe my family had become. Were we right to get rid of Boomer and get Sam to choose another dog right away? Would that help him move on or just give him other scars, ones we couldn't see?

I was clueless.

ROSE PLANNED OPERATION PUPPY POWER with a precision that made a Swiss watch look disorganized. We would rendezvous at the American Kennels pet store, 798 Lexington Avenue, GPS coordinates 40.763785,-73.966921, at 1200 hours.

(Rose's intel had it on deep background that this was the pet store at which Mary-Kate Olsen had bought her Labrador retriever.) There we would meet Rose's contact, code name "Harold," who would whisk Sam to a secure location—a loft area above the store—where prescreened pugs (chosen for their small size and well-researched child-friendliness) would be brought to Sam for interrogation and possible love-match. I would be up in the interrogation loft with Sam while Rose, balancing Benny on one hip as she scouted potential friendlies with Harold, was our person on the ground.

Subject number one was a tiny bit of fawn-colored fluff, a brand-spanking-new, whelped-that-morning pug puppy, so cute you wanted to kill it. I scratched it behind its velvet-soft ears and placed it in Sam's lap.

"Whadya think, huh, buddy? Totally, really, unbelievably cute, huh? Huh?" I said, nodding and smiling in that way peculiar to desperate parents. Sam, on the cusp of four, looked at me with his world-weary eyes, and then looked at the puppy in his lap and then said, "Dad?"

"Yeah, buddy?"

"I don't like this dog."

"Whadya mean, buddy?"

"I mean, I don't like this dog."

"How come, pal?"

"Kinda looks like a rat."

I don't know how long I sat there with that dumb smile frozen on my face, but it seemed like forever.

"That's okay, we'll get you another one, okay? Okay?"

Sam just looked down at his hands, saying nothing, until I placed another candidate into them. Another pug puppy, but older and, I hoped, less ratlike in Sam's estimation.

Sam looked up at me, shaking his head. "Dad, I told you. I don't like this dog."

"But this one's bigger, not rat-like at all, see?"

Sam rolled his eyes.

"I'm gonna talk to the guy," he said, going over my head. He knocked on the glass of the window overlooking the pet store to get the attention of the salesman (and everybody else in the store).

"Hey! Hey, guy!"

"Sam, the man has a name. His name is Harold, okay?"

"Okay," he said, knocking on the glass again, even louder this time. "Hey, Harold!"

Harold looked up at the balcony quizzically, somewhat bemused to be addressed by a preschooler in such a commanding way.

"Harold! I don't like this dog! It looks like a rat!"

Harold looked at me and I looked at my shoes. This was not going, even remotely, according to plan.

"I want THAT one!" Sam finally yelled.

I cringed. We thought a pug would be a good choice because they were both child- and apartment-friendly. With my luck, Sam had just picked out either a Saint Bernard or a Komodo dragon. Thankfully, it was merely a feloniously overpriced French bulldog.

"I love this dog!" Sam said, promptly dubbing it Spike, after the bulldog in the *Tom and Jerry* cartoons. Even though little Miss Spike cost roughly four times what we'd planned to spend, I didn't argue. She'd put the first smile on Sam's face I had seen since the dog bite.

SAM ALSO LOVED FAO SCHWARZ, toy store of all toy stores and the next stop on Rose's shock-and-awe, make-Sam-think-getting-bitten-in-the-face-was-the-best-thing-that-ever-happened-to-him tour—at least until I insisted that we make a pit stop to apply medicine to his wound before moving on to the ice cream parlor, our next stop on the tour.

"Can't it wait until we get home?" Rose asked.

I looked over at Sam, happily playing foosball with Rose. It seemed a shame to pull him away when he was obviously having so much fun. But the doctor had said we needed to check the stitches and apply the antibacterial ointment every four hours, and wasn't it not sweating small stuff like applying medicine on time and training dogs off beds that had gotten us into this particular mess?

"No," I said. I was going to learn from our mistakes. I owed Sam that much, at the very least. I pulled Sam away from the foosball game, and he reluctantly followed me into the men's room at the toy store. I lifted him up on the sink and gave him my best "this won't hurt a bit" smile as I gingerly pulled off the gauze bandage covering his stitches. They looked great. No redness or discharge. Everything shipshape.

That's when I noticed the look of horror on Sam's face and realized that this was the first time he'd actually seen his wound uncovered. All my efforts to be conscientious, learn my lesson, take care of his wound on schedule, had just led to this horrible image being his memory of the toy store that day.

"Dad, they made me a zipper!" he said, staring at the stitches, looking like crooked Frankenstein train tracks down the center of his nose.

"I'm a zipper!" he said again, horrified.

"No, you're not. The stitches will come out soon, don't worry. You're not a zipper, you're . . . brave. You're the bravest boy."

"Why'd this have to happen?! Why?!" he cried, burying his face in my shoulder.

There was no good answer to this question. The truth, that this was my fault, would kill him like a dog. As much as I wanted to confess to him, to have him forgive me, to do so would take away the one strong shoulder he thought he could cry on.

"You're the bravest boy," I repeated, not knowing what else to say.

"I don't wanna be brave!" he cried.

Me neither, kid. Me neither.

Chapter Fourteen

DOWN THE MOUNTAIN

THE BOMBER was made for roads like this. The twisty ribbon of fresh asphalt corkscrewed its way down the northern face of the Blue Ridge Mountains. We were near that point on the map where Virginia nudges up against Pennsylvania and the Southeast United States gives way abruptly to the Northeast. We'd spent the night near Roanoke, Virginia, and would be in New York by sundown. Dad held on to his seat as I redlined my way down the mountain, leaning into curves with my foot dancing between the brake and the accelerator, downshifting to keep the Bomber's big V8 in the torquey sweet spot around 3,500 rpms. The throaty rumble of the engine was music to my ears, and the kiss of the wide tires on the hot asphalt a physical pleasure. This was sweetheart driving—I didn't know where I stopped and the car began.

"Handles like a dream—especially for a big car," I said.

"Is it that much bigger than your last BMW?" Dad asked.

"It *better* be," I said, smiling. "That was my whole rationalization to Rose for why we needed to get another car so soon."

"When'd you get that last one?"

"About a year ago," I said. "We got Speedy right after . . . " My voice trailed off as we leaned into the next curve. We got Speedy during that same shock-and-awe week of positive distractions after the dog bite that had included Sam's trips to the pet store and FAO Schwarz. Sam got a new puppy and I got a new car. Maybe the only difference between men and boys really is just the size of their toys. I know it doesn't seem fair—Sam was the one who got hurt, why should *I* get a car out of the deal?

In my defense, please let the record show that the whole thing was Rose's idea.

"I want a BMW," Rose said to me the night after we brought home Sam's new puppy.

"What?" I said, pulling off the pillow I'd placed over my head to drown out the puppy's whining so I could get some sleep.

"I think we should get a BMW," Rose repeated.

I was instantly WIDE AWAKE—if you're a frustrated car guy, having your wife tell you she wants a BMW is almost like having the lady in your life tell you she wants to try a three-way.

"The only reason we got the Volkswagen van is to have space for Boomer and Bailey," she explained. "With them gone, it feels like we're driving a hearse. We had this BMW when I was a little girl that ran forever. I always felt safe in it. I just want to feel safe again."

I hastily agreed. What a guy.

That was the night that BMW became more than just the

"ultimate driving machine." Somehow the car became almost a prayer, to just feel safe again, to have a fresh start on the road of life. We couldn't afford a new BMW, so, as Rose slept fitfully next to me, I stayed up late searching online for the ultimate "like new" driving machine, hoping somehow that it would help us feel like new again too. I know, it sounds desperate, stupid—but that's how stupid desperate we were. I would have put our life savings into an almighty toaster at that point.

Finally, in the wee hours of that morning, I came across a promising 1998 5 Series on AutoTrader: only 17,179 miles . . . driven by an honest-to-God little old lady . . . in Florida . . . being sold by her son who was, frosting-on-the-cake, a mechanic. Baby, I was gone. I called the seller, out in Kutztown, Pennsylvania, in the morning and struck a deal. He would even take our Volkswagen van as a trade-in.

We were late getting on the road that day, and by the time we got through New York City traffic and out to Kutztown, where the mechanic son was storing Speedy in his garage, it was well after dark. Switching cars in the middle of nowhere, under the cover of night, made me feel like we were fugitives, a family on the lam. I joked about this to Rose, but she didn't laugh. It was too close to the truth.

On the way back to New York after picking up Speedy that night, I told Sam that Speedy was our getaway car, the fastest car in the world. To every car we passed, he would joyfully shout out "See ya!" I was grateful to hear him laugh again. I looked back in the rearview mirror. Sam has a dazzling this-kid-could-be-president-someday smile, but all I could see that night were the fresh stitches running down his nose like a crooked zipper. Our eyes met in the mirror. It takes the coordinated effort of thirteen separate muscles in your face to smile. For his sake, I did my best to pull it off.

I told myself we would be fine. The universe was out of other shoes to drop on us. We just needed a vacation, a chance to get away. A month in the country. The idyllic vacation property Rose found in Connecticut was, literally, something out of a magazine.

"It's so perfect! Just look at these pictures!" Rose said, her voice high-pitched, I guess with excitement, but something about it reminded me of how characters in bad movies talk when they're secretly being held hostage and have to pretend everything is a-okay. As Rose handed me the pictures, I noticed that the tendons in her arm and neck were as taut as the strings of an overtuned guitar, one more twist away from snapping. Rose smiled at me, bravely, desperately, almost begging me not to do my usual harrumphing about how we couldn't afford anything.

"It looks lovely," I said, not bothering to look at the pictures. Rose couldn't afford *not* to have a month in the country. We would pay for it somehow.

AS BEAUTIFUL AS THE PICTURES WERE, they just didn't do justice to all the lovely details that made our five-acre farm retreat such a special place to take young children: the treehouse equipped with clever, easy-to-leave-open trapdoors, the inviting frog pond just deep enough to drown in, the quaint potting shed chock-full of brightly colored insecticide containers, and, my personal favorite, the steep colonial stairways tailor-made for the cleaving of toddler's skulls.

These amenities gave Rose, already at wit's end, a whole new lease on anxiety. She became the MacGyver of all Jewish mothers. She could take a few simple items—a hairpin, a glass of water, a toaster oven—and easily improvise half-a-dozen household accidents, each capable of wiping out our entire family.

Dad and my brother Paul joined us for a lovely week there in our white-knuckle retreat. In the months since my mother passed, we'd had a few mini-reunions like this. I hate to say it, but life, at least our family life, was easier—if a lot less interesting—now that she was gone. One day while Dad and Paul were with us in Connecticut, Sam ran into the kitchen from outside, breathless with excitement.

"Grandpa let me ride in the front seat of the car like a big boy!" he gushed to all assembled. I looked up from trying to coax more puréed chicken-and-dumplings dinner into Benny in his high chair. Paul, seated on the other side of the kitchen table, just grunted, too engrossed with his speed-reading a book on something called Reiki. (Paul had been working his way through my mother's collection of New Age books since she passed.) Rose stood in the door to our bedroom, bristling with rage.

"Grandpa let you ride in the *front seat* of the car?" Rose said, trying to keep her cool as Dad sauntered in looking modest, his hands full of grocery bags from his trip to town with Sam.

"Yeah! Like a big boy!" Sam said, beaming.

"You shouldn't ride in the front seat, it's dangerous," Rose said.

"Airbags," I explained to Dad.

"Sorry, been a while since I had young ones," Dad said. "Didn't have the airbags back then."

"It's *dangerous* to have him sit in the front seat," Rose repeated.

"Grandpa's dangerous?" Sam asked, his big eyes all on me.

"It's just that it's safer in the backseat, that's all Mom meant."

"Okay," Sam said. "I'll ride in the backseat when we go to Grandma Carole's house."

Say what?

"Grandma Carole's house?" I asked.

"Yeah! Grandpa John said that on account of a re-in-t-tarnation—"

"Re-in-*car*-nation," Paul corrected, looking up from his Reiki book.

"Reincarnation, yeah—on account of that, Grandma Carole's alive again and living in somebody else's house! Can we go there now?"

"That was *quite* the trip to town, Dad," I said. "I ask you to pick up sunscreen and you come back with *reincarnation*?"

"Well, at least as many people in the world believe in some form of reincarnation as do the heaven/hell construct of Judeo-Christian faiths," Paul said.

"You're taking *his* side?" I snapped at Paul before turning to Dad for his explanation.

"Well, on the way back from Price Chopper—"

"With Sam in the *front seat*—" Rose said under her breath for all to hear.

"I can handle this," I said.

"*Can* you?" Rose jabbed.

"When do we get to go to Grandma's house?" Sam asked.

"Ahhh . . . Grandpa's talking right now, please don't interrupt," I said, vamping for time. I needed a moment before I was ready to confront the afterlife with Sam.

"Well, everybody *else* is interrupting," Sam said, kicking the leg of Benny's high chair, which, of course, made Benny cry.

"Careful!" Rose yelled to make Sam stop—which just made Benny cry louder.

"Everybody just listen to Grandpa," I said, picking up Benny to comfort him. "He's going to explain how he turned sunscreen into reincarnation."

Dad sighed, looking pained—his equivalent of hitting the roof.

"Well, on the way back from the Price Chopper," he began again, "Sam started talking about missing Carole and I said that I did too, and he wanted to know where you go when you die, and I said that different people believed different things and that Grandma Carole believed in reincarnation, and he said, 'What's reincarnation?' and so I explained it to him—"

"To a four-year-old?" I said, incredulously.

"I'm four and a half!" Sam protested. "I wanna go to Grandma's house!"

"No, Sam," I said.

"I wanna go NOW!" Sam wailed, jumping up and down as Benny, still hungry, screamed in my ear for more chicken and dumplings.

"No!"

"Why not?!"

"Because Grandma's not in some house somewhere, she's just dead, okay? She's dead!"

Silence.

It's never as quiet as that shocked instant right before a kid starts to bawl his head off.

"*Waaaaaaaaaaaaaaaaaaa!!*"

I just stared at the floor as Sam ran off to his room and slammed the door. I congratulated myself—I had just presided over his Grandma being killed a second time.

"I . . . I can't deal with this!" Rose said, throwing up her hands.

As she retreated into our room and slammed the door, I pictured my mother looking down on this scene from somewhere up there in "reintarnation" and having a good laugh.

"Well . . . that didn't go very well," Paul finally said.

"Thanks for pointing that out, bro," I said.

"Can I do anything?" Dad asked.

"I think you've done enough," I said, shaking my head.

"*Daddy, I want you!*" Sam cried from up in his room.

I sighed and handed Benny to Dad. "Here, try not to break him."

"BUT IF GRANDMA'S JUST DEAD, then I'll never get to see her again!" Sam sobbed, hugging his knees in a fetal position on the bed.

"Well, ah . . . she's not *just* dead. She's . . . she's . . . "

"In heaven?" Sam asked.

"That's right," I said. "Grandma Carole is in heaven." As a lapsed Unitarian, I pretty much had carte blanche to opt for whatever version of the afterlife seemed most politically expedient.

Sam stopped crying.

"Will *I* go to heaven?"

"Of *course* you will, and then you can be with Grandma Carole forever," I said—even though this might be closer to my personal idea of hell than heaven.

Sam thought about this.

"Will *you* go to heaven?"

"Um . . . sure. All the good people get to go."

"*All* of them?"

"Yeah."

Sam thought about this for a moment and then started to cry all over again.

"*What*, buddy?" I said, hugging him.

"Well, it's just that . . . heaven sounds *really* crowded. What if I can't find you?"

I shook my head. The daddy-pants were way too big for me. I was drowning in them.

"**SAM'S BETTER NOW,**" I said to Rose.

She raised a finger, finishing up a phone call.

I had found her where I always did—curled up in bed and at work at the same time. At times, she can remind me of the worst parts of both my parents: a workaholic who was, at the same time, in full retreat from the world.

"What did you say to him?" she asked after she hung up.

"That Grandma was in heaven. And that the cool thing about heaven is that they give you walkie-talkies so you can always find each other."

Rose didn't crack a smile.

"I need to go back to work," she said, reaching for the phone once more. Her ability to keep dotting her i's and crossing her t's at work while falling apart at home truly amazed me.

"Come on, this is our vacation. You shouldn't be working," I said.

"Someone has to pay for all this."

"But what's the point of being in this fancy place if you can't enjoy it? Come on, we're gonna jump in the pool—"

"Did your father get the sunscreen?"

"Yeah," I said, handing it to her.

"This is only SPF 40—I asked him to get the SPF 50."

"What difference does it make, it's sunscreen."

"It's our *son*, we have to keep his scar covered with the highest sunscreen so it will heal, that's what the doctor said!"

"Just relax, okay? Come out to the pool, take a swim."

"I can't, I have a migraine," she said, popping two of her headache horse-pills. Whether or not these pills really took away her headache was academic because after she took them, she was gone.

"Don't you think you should take those with some food?"

"I'll just throw it up."

"Come on, just a bagel or something."

"I ate yesterday," she said, pushing her hair, shockingly gray at the roots, out of her face to sip some Coca-Cola to help settle her stomach.

"Honey, please—you need to see somebody, a doctor."

"I feel too sick to go see a doctor," she said, suppressing a retch.

"Too sick to see a doctor? Do you know how crazy that sounds?"

"Stop beating up on me!"

"Honey, I . . . I just want to help you. Tell me what you need."

"I . . . I just need . . . I just need the sunscreen."

"The sunscreen?"

"For Sam. Will you get it before he goes in the pool? Will you promise me?"

"Honey, you can't keep going on like this. I can't take it."

"Well, I'm sorry I'm such a burden."

"Honey, please—I can't deal with you when you get like this."

"Well, this is who I am, okay? If you can't deal with it, then maybe we don't belong together. Maybe I should just go."

Then, as I am prone to do at the most inappropriate moments, I laughed. "Honey, you keep threatening to leave me, but you're too sick to get out of bed. I'm sorry, but if you really want to scare me, you're gonna have to raise your game a little."

"That was mean. The man I married wasn't mean. I don't know who you are anymore . . . " she said, her voice trailing off, which was just as well. When she started saying things I couldn't bear to hear, I just tuned her out anyway. She had become background noise for me at this point, elevator music in an elevator that only went down. I squinted at the sunscreen label in the dark of the migraine room, trying to figure out what the hell SPF stood for anyway.

"Well, I'm gonna go," I said.

"You're going to leave?" she asked, a sense of urgency cutting through the haze between us.

"Ah . . . yeah."

"You're leaving me," she said again in a voice both shaky and, oddly, relieved. As if she always knew it would come to this.

"I'm leaving you *to get the sunscreen*, okay? Everything is *fine*. Please attempt to chill," I said, grabbing my car keys.

IF YOUR FAMILY IS FALLING APART emotionally, the very least you can do is handle it like a man: Tell yourself everything is fine—and then figure out some excuse for getting out of the house. That's what real men do. That's what my father did, and, without realizing it, I learned his lesson well. Rose found the regularity with which we ran out of sunscreen during our month in the country simply astounding. And how was it possible that my runs to the store always took at least an hour even though town was just ten minutes away?

Well, you had to work at it.

My favorite route took Speedy and me far into the next county and all the way around Lake Waramaug. The twisty country roads of rural Connecticut, especially when driving Speedy a healthy twenty miles per hour over the speed limit, gave me a much needed jolt of *farfegnugen*:

> farfegnugen—n., a speed-induced euphoric state in which the driver of an automobile believes he/she is moving at a sufficient rate of speed to leave all troubles behind. Also see DENIAL.

After our month in the country that summer, we took Speedy on a number of other getaways. Every place was different and yet they were all the same—just someplace new and different to have the same old issues.

"DOES THIS CAR HANDLE like your other BMW did?" Dad asked

I blinked, wondering how many turns I had taken lost in the windshield, reflecting on the vacation that wasn't.

"What?" I asked.

"Is it the same driving this BMW as the last one or is it different?"

I shook my head, realizing there was no magic getaway car fast enough for us to outrun our past. I had switched cars and the scenery had changed, but I hadn't moved forward. I was still driving in circles around Lake Waramaug, fooling myself with farfegnugen, not daring to look in the rearview mirror because in it was only pain and the warning that objects in the mirror were closer than they appeared.

"It's the same," I finally said. "It's exactly the same."

My big road trip was coming to an end and I had nothing for my family, not even souvenirs.

The car was empty.

Chapter Fifteen

THE LINCOLN TUNNEL

DAD AND I had made it down the majestic mountains of Virginia, across a quaint patch of Pennsylvania Dutch Country, and through the cluster-fuck of chemical plants and cloverleafs that is the Garden State of New Jersey. We were now—as we had been for the last half hour—just minutes away from entering the Lincoln Tunnel.

"You'll be here *tomorrow*? As in the day after today? *That* tomorrow you're talking?" Nick, the AC guy, said over the phone when I gave him my E.T.A.

"I'll actually be back in the city today but just to drop off my dad at Penn Station and then I drive upstate to get my family. We should be back in the city tomorrow around noon. You'll be done by then, right?"

"In a word—*no fucking way*. They just got the new breaker box wired up yesterday, I've been hooking up your ducts and whatnot, but I couldn't hook up the compressor without the box. My hands were tied here."

"Is the place a huge mess? Is there a lot of dust?" I asked, trying to stay calm.

"Um, define *a lot*," came his less than reassuring reply.

"Look, I told you, my wife has killer asthma. If there's a lot of dust, she'll have a heart attack and kill me."

"From beyond the grave?" Nick asked.

"You don't know my wife. She's capable, I'm telling you."

"I'll send flowers," Nick said. "Now, if you don't mind, I got work to do."

"Everything okay?" Dad asked as I tossed my cell phone onto the dash.

"Um, define *okay*," I said.

I tried not to feel Dad's concerned gaze as I stared out the windshield at the bottleneck between us and the entrance to the tunnel. Stop-and-go death by inches. The pulse of traffic growing steadily weaker. It reminded me of watching helplessly as Mom's heart ticked down.

I chuckled, mirth-free, congratulating myself on one of my more existential moods.

Honk!!! Honk!!! Honk!!!

That would be the big red Hummer that had been merging on me for the last several minutes without so much as a right turn signal. Just letting me know whose bitch I was as he finally squeezed in front of me.

"Congratulations, you're an asshole," I said, giving the red Hummer a double-fisted middle-finger salute.

"Won't be long now," Dad said, with the congenital patience of a true Midwesterner.

"Yeah," I said, feeling oddly ambivalent about that fact. I actually envied the red Hummer. That asshole had someplace he wanted to be so badly he was willing to fight dirty every inch of the way to get there. I was feeling the furthest thing from farfegnugen at the moment. They seem to have a word for everything in German, so they must have a single, Germanically precise word for the existential claustrophobia one experiences when stuck in traffic en route to a destination at which you would rather not arrive. Four days on the road and I still wasn't ready to be home. Not ready to face that music.

Without the new air conditioning system, I imagined our apartment feeling like my parents' house back in Virginia. My parents didn't believe in air conditioning. They were children of the Depression and still somehow regarded air conditioning with skepticism, at odds with their belief that life was to be endured, not enjoyed. Air conditioning could break down, whereas an ability to suffer was something you could put stock in, like U. S. Steel. On long summer days, the air in my parents' house weighed on you like the blanket of a sickbed, comforting and suffocating at the same time, heavy with a whole time machine of smells—a tuna casserole from back in the Carter Administration when my parents had first moved to Virginia; the pee of three generations of housecat, all named Spritzer, all long dead; the acrid turpentine from the last time Mom ever let Dad clean his paintbrushes in the house; my mother's perfume; my father's Head & Shoulders.

The house was watched over by papier-mâché angels that I had made everyone for Christmas back when I was short on money but

long on time. They were artistic, earnest failures—the worst kind—
that only a mother could love. That and simple neglect kept them
displayed, pushpinned to the ceiling, hanging over us like the memory of all our good intentions.

The home that waited for me on the other side of the tunnel felt
achingly familiar, like the one I grew up in. A place where the walls
closed in, where everything went unsaid until the air there was as
thick with recriminations and blame as the air here at the mouth of
the Lincoln Tunnel was with exhaust fumes and road rage. Even
when the new air conditioning system was up and running, it
wouldn't clear that air for my family.

"They were never the same after that."

That's what I imagined our friends and neighbors would say
about us if I didn't find a way to patch things up with Rose. There
was no real rhyme or reason for everything that had happened to
us, but still, we must find answers. And if I wanted to find the
answers, I had to be willing to ask the questions.

"How come you didn't make Mom get help?" I asked Dad, apro-
pos of nothing and everything.

He didn't flinch, didn't raise an eyebrow. This made me sad for
him. If questions like this came as no surprise, it must mean that
they were already on his mind. I wondered, how well did I even
know my father? What screaming doubts had he borne silently all
these years? What self-criticisms had rattled around in his head as
he nodded and smiled for the rest of us to see?

"You can't *make* someone get help," he finally said.

"But what if you have to?"

"That was all really your mother's area," he said.

"Her area?"

"Psychological things. The emotional aspect of life. I just . . . provided. Stood by her. That's all I knew to do. It wasn't enough, clearly . . . "

Dad looked out his window, studied one of the eighteen wheels of the semitrailer merging in next to us. Its air brakes gave a mournful yelp as it inched forward.

"Dad, I'm not criticizing you."

This made him turn to look at me.

"Dad, if I'd known how hard it was to be a husband and a father, I would've tried to be a better son."

Dad smiled and we both turned to look out the windshield, studying the bumper of the red asshole Hummer in front of us as the traffic pulsed forward again. I let the 18-wheeler slide in front of me. I wasn't ready for this road trip to end. Not ready to say good-bye to my dad.

"I'm scared, Dad," I said, my own words surprising me as they left my mouth. Why is it that the truth always feels like a surprise? He turned to look at me.

"What about?" he asked.

"I'm scared for my boys." It was harder to admit this to myself than to him.

"Well, you got that speech therapist for Benny and that plastic surgeon for Sam. You're doing all you can."

"Oh Dad, that's the least of it. I'm afraid that . . . " I gripped the steering wheel white-knuckle tight even though we weren't going anywhere, just trying to hold on, but the words came out anyway.

"I'm afraid they're going to grow up in an unhappy home like I did."

That's a hell of a thing to say to your father. How's a man

supposed to hear that? I'm sure many men would fly into a rage or tell me to stop whining or just stop talking to me. Forever.

But my dad just nodded.

"I'm sorry, Dad, it's just Rose—she's not getting better. I don't know what to do for her, so I . . . I just go to work like you did—"

"You're not me. You're not going to make the same mistakes I did."

"But Dad, Rose and I . . . " I said, shaking my head. "What the hell do I do?"

Dad bowed his head, thinking long and hard—this was for all the marbles.

"Son, I don't know."

I studied the dead bugs on the windshield. While I respected my father's honesty, I was really hoping he'd have something a little more Oprah-worthy for me at this moment. The tunnel swallowed the 18-wheeler ahead of us. It wouldn't be long now.

Dad cleared his throat.

"But I do know this—when the time comes, *you* will know what to do. I do know that. I could have never handled the things that happened to you all the way you did. You . . . you're more of a man than I ever was. You were there when they needed you. You just trust yourself. You'll know what's right."

Such a sweet thing for my dad to say. Wrong, of course, but sweet.

We entered the tunnel.

Chapter Sixteen

HOME SWEET HOME

THE GOOSE PIMPLES streaked up my arm like a fuse being lit.

I shivered. There was an ice cream tingle in the air, courtesy of our new central-air system. *Quiet.* Just the arctic breath of some abominable snowman on my face. A thin layer of white plaster dust blanketed our living room like make-believe snow in some department-store winter wonderland, but Santa was nowhere to be seen. Just Nick, AC guy extraordinaire, hands on hips, proudly filthy from his labors. Nothing more cleansing than work that gets you dirty.

"You're lucky I don't charge extra for miracles," he said. "Worked half the night getting the system up and juiced for you."

"I appreciate it," I said. "Sure is nice and cool."

"*Cool?* It's a *popsicle factory* in here. And I put up some plastic to contain the dust from that little bit of ripping apart your whole ceiling I had to do for the ducts."

"Thank you," Rose said, as chilly as the air. If she remained as cold to me as she'd been since I picked up her and the boys at Saul and Ruth's place, I would never have to worry about air conditioning again.

She walked quickly past us to take refuge in our bedroom on the other side of the plastic curtain.

"Who's this little guy?" Nick said to Benny, who was shyly peaking from behind me.

I smiled the idiot smile of all proud fathers while I waited what seemed like forever for Benny to talk.

"Come on, you know your name, just let me hear you say it," I finally said.

Benny didn't like the way this conversation was going. He emphatically lifted his arms and grunted for me to pick him up.

"This chatterbox is Benny," I said, hoisting him. "And this is his brother, Sam."

Sam politely shook Nick's hand and then turned to me. "Dad, Spike peed on the rug."

"*Already?* We just got here!" I took one step toward the little black-and-white dog and then, either from anxiety or just to spite me, the precious mutt promptly peed again.

Deep breath.

While I understood the therapeutic need for Sam to have this dog, I also understood that *I* would need a lot of therapy not to want to kill it every time it went "makey" in the house. I have dog issues.

"Will you clean it up, please?" I asked Sam.

"Um . . . I'm pretty sure Mom needs me?" he said, beating a hasty retreat from clean-up duty.

"You're *pretty sure*, huh?" I said with a chuckle, enjoying his work.

"I'll go check," Sam helpfully suggested and promptly disappeared.

"Ready for the nickel tour?" Nick asked, climbing a ladder up to a crawl space that housed the guts of our new central air.

I gently pried Benny off me and sat him down on the couch.

"Da-da!"

"It's okay, I'm just going to climb up on this ladder so Nick can show me something."

Benny did *not* approve. He shook his head using his whole body the way only a two-year-old can.

"Just a second," I said, climbing up the ladder.

"Da-da!"

"Don't worry, Daddy's going to be safe."

"DA-DA!"

I squeezed into the crawl space next to Nick.

"Okay, Mr. Mark, up here's where you change the filter—"

"DA-DA YOU DOWN!"

I didn't believe my ears. I poked my head out of the crawl space to see Benny standing on the couch, his little kid face so gravely serious it made me smile.

"Benny, did you . . . *say* something?" Rose said, coming out from our bedroom.

"DA-DA YOU DOWN!" he screamed again in a shriek that could peel paint. After waiting so long to hear him talk, it was the most beautiful sound in the world.

"Okay, Benny. I heard you. I'm coming down."

I climbed down the ladder and Rose scooped up Benny and held him tight. Her eyes met mine and I had the strangest sensation, one I hadn't had in what seemed like forever—I recognized my wife. All the worry lines that for so long had obscured her face like scaffold-ing were gone in this moment of relief.

"I remember you," I said to Rose, and she smiled.

"Good job, Benny!" she cooed, squeezing him so tight I was afraid he'd break.

"How come if *I* yell, I just get in trouble?" Sam asked, and we all laughed so hard that Rose, for once, didn't hear her cell phone ring.

"It was the office," she said, looking at the caller ID.

"Can it wait?" I asked, not wanting this moment to end.

"Well . . . " she said, casting her eyes around the room, "it'll just take a moment and besides I . . . I really shouldn't be out here in all this dust."

"Of course, the dust," I said. She retreated to our bedroom to call her office, and the bubble of that perfect moment burst as quickly and unexpectedly as it had formed.

AFTER NICK LEFT THAT NIGHT, I cleaned and cleaned, attacking the dust. Here, at last, was something I could do. To make Rose feel safe in her own house, in her own skin. To finally make us clean of everything that had happened. The dust clung to every-thing. The priceless and the worthless alike. The public spaces yielded most easily. Floors were easily swept and mopped. Carpets could be vacuumed. Even upholstery could be beaten dust-free if you put your back into it.

It was the private spaces, the forgotten, out-of-sight jumbles hid-den in closets and drawers, that took real doing. We have a hall closet where everything gets thrown. All junk and soon-to-be-junk.

It was a compost heap of memory—enough time in the hall closet will break down any keepsake, no matter how dear, to mere junk and dust. I read somewhere that most household dust is just tiny pieces of ourselves. We die a little every day, shedding our skin in tiny particles that accumulate, like sand through the hourglass, to mark the passing of our days. From dust thou art and unto dust thou shalt return.

Undaunted, into the depths of the hall closet I went, facing down a rogue's gallery of old sports equipment, the ghosts of Christmases past in the form of gifts we meant to return or neglected to give, and a whole orphanage of broken and forgotten toys. It was here, in the depths of the hall closet, that I struck gold, buried treasure—a time capsule of happier days. I found us or, rather, "WE"—the first installment of my ill-fated grand plan to take each word from a short, clumsily written poem I'd penned for our wedding vows and illustrate it with keepsakes from the past year.

Only three years into our marriage and three words into the poem, life got too nuts to fulfill my grand design, leaving us with: WE—HAVE—NOTHING. But none of that history was written when I put together "WE" for our first anniversary. In it was all our idealism, all our hope—a sprig from Rose's bridal bouquet, pictures of our wedding, paint swatches from Bailey Farm, even one of the goofy postcards I'd sent Rose back when we were courting. It was all there, everything that was most essential to us, all safe, encased in bubble wrap all this time. Finding it at that moment felt like finding the Rosebud sled in *Citizen Kane* in time to spare it from the ashes.

"Rose!" I yelled, coughing from the dust, as I tried to wrest "WE" from the clutter of the hall closet without falling off my stepladder.

"You won't believe what I found! Come here!"

I got tangled up in the cord of an old paint-spattered radio I use when renovating and lost my balance on the stepladder. I slammed my elbow into the wall rather than dropping the "WE." *Why do they call it the funny bone when hitting it is anything but?* Smarting from that, I did not see the little present Spike had left me there on the floor of the hall. I was barefoot. The green-brown feces oozed between my toes.

"Spike!" I bellowed.

"What's the special surprise, Dad?!" Sam asked.

"In a minute!" I spit out, leaving "WE" on the floor next to the dog shit to hunt down the little mutt and teach it a lesson. I hobbled like a pirate, walking on the heel of my dog-shit foot to avoid tracking the mess all over the apartment. In my peg-legged fury, you'd think I was hunting the great white whale instead of this little black-and-white dog. I found the beast deep below the surface of the couch. It writhed like a fish as I grabbed it by the scruff of the neck and Ahab'd my way back to the scene of the crime.

"BAD DOG!" I yelled, rubbing Spike's nose in her mess and smacking her on the butt en route to tossing her in the bathroom and slamming the door. Only then, when the dog's yelping finally died down, did I hear the crying coming from the master bedroom.

My feet knew that the cries belonged to Sam and commenced to flat-out run, my dog-shit foot squishing across the hardwood floor to the other side of the apartment. Sam came out of our bedroom, his face horrible with tears as he ran to his room and slammed the door.

"What happened?"

"When you yelled at the dog it reminded Sam of—" Rose shook her head involuntarily, the way you do when you catch a chill, a gesture that had come to mean, in the unfortunate shorthand of our family, "the dog bite."

I nodded.

"He said he wanted Boomer to come back. That it was his fault that Boomer had to go away."

"He thinks it's *his* fault?"

"I told him it wasn't. That it was *my* fault because I told him to jump up on the bed and then he screamed and ran into his room," she said numbly, as if talking about something she'd seen on the news. It's the things closest to home that we have to hold at arm's length.

"It is Mom's fault?" Sam moaned after I got to his room.

"No," I said.

He cried only louder.

"Then it *is* my fault!"

I shook my head. He needed an answer. To understand what happened to him. Our guilt had prevented us from giving him a proper one.

"No, Sam," I finally said. "It wasn't your fault. I never want you to think that."

"Then whose fault was it?"

"What if it's no one's fault?" I said, thinking aloud.

"Then why'd it happen? Why'd Boomer bite me?"

"Well, ah . . . that's a good question. It was a really dumb thing for him to do."

"Don't say dumb," Sam corrected me just as I had corrected him in the past. It's scary what sponges children are, how even our off-the-cuff comments get sucked up by them and are made gospel. No pressure. I swallowed.

"Well, you're right. Dumb isn't a nice word, but the truth is that dogs just aren't smart like you are. I mean . . . Spike can't even tell the difference between inside and outside, that's why she keeps making messes in the house. It can be really frustrating, but I shouldn't have yelled the way I did. I'm sorry."

"It's okay."

"And Boomer, he . . . he always thought he was a little dog. Remember the funny way he used to hide behind me and get all nervous?"

"Yeah."

"And so, when you jumped on the bed, he got scared because he thought you were a big dog."

"He *did*?" Sam seemed tickled at the idea of being the big dog.

"Yeah. And *that's* why he bit you—because he thought you were a big dog and he was a little dog and so he had to defend himself. Isn't that silly? But dogs aren't like people—people can learn things. They can grow and change," I said.

I wasn't sure if this last thing was really true or not.

But I hoped so.

"YOU WERE IN THERE A LONG TIME. Is he okay?" Rose asked when I had finally emerged.

"He's good. He just wanted me to stay with him until he went to sleep."

"What did you say to him?"

"I just explained to him that the bite was no one's fault, that Boomer didn't mean to hurt him, it's just that dogs aren't very smart. And then he wanted me to go through every single pet I ever had, including the pet rock I had when I was four, and tell him what life lesson they failed to learn," I said with a yawn.

"You're Super Daddy," Rose said, doing something on her laptop.

"Well, you and I both know that's not true, but I'd like to spare him the rude awakening. At least until he's six. What're you doing?"

"I'm just on eBay."

"You're *shopping*?"

"I know, you're Super Daddy and I just go shopping. I just felt bad and I wanted to get him something. Is there anything wrong with that?"

"I guess not," I said. "What'd you get him?"

"Baseball cards."

"Baseball cards?"

"Yeah. It took me forever, but I found him a complete set for the '86 Mets."

"Honey, that's great, but I just don't know if the answer to all our problems is baseball cards."

"What do you mean—*all our problems*?"

"I was talking about the baseball cards."

"Then why'd you say *we have problems*?"

"Well, *clearly* we have problems, honey. And if you really think you can just lie in bed and buy a few baseball cards and that's going to make everything all better, then we *really* have problems."

"You feel like a big man yelling at the little dog and scaring your children half to death?"

"Hey, I helped him tonight. What I said really comforted him—"

"Of course it did. You're Super Daddy."

I shook my head, started to back out of the room. I needed to take a walk.

"What is it you wanted to show me?"

"What?" I said, stopping.

"Before the whole night went to shit, you said you found something in the closet."

I looked out the door of our room to the "WE" lying on the ground next to the dog shit.

"Nothing," I finally said. "Nevermind."

"NO, DAD—WALLY BACKMAN played second base on the '86 Mets and Ray Knight goes on third base," Sam said, moving these players' baseball cards to their proper positions on an impromptu baseball diamond we had set up on the carpet of the plastic surgeon's waiting room.

"What the heck was I thinking?" I said, trying not to feel too annoyed at how right Rose had been about Sam loving these darn baseball cards. Since the cards arrived a week ago, he'd played with them nonstop. She also got him a DVD boxed set of the '86 Miracle Mets World Series against Boston that he watched endlessly, reenacting the key plays using the baseball cards like we were doing now.

"Jesse Orosco pitches and . . . he strikes out Marty Barrett! He struck him out! The Mets win the World Series!"

"The doctor will see you now," said a nurse wearing green scrubs. The scrubs surprised me. Rose had set up this appointment—just for a "treatment," she said. Why was the nurse dressed for surgery?

I had a sinking feeling as Sam and I picked up the baseball cards.

"YOUR SON WON'T BE IN PAIN," the doctor said. "It'll all be over in seconds."

And then, he smiled.

I just looked at the guy, at his straight white teeth. I didn't trust him. I knew doctors—too many of them—and, in my experience, it was not one of the smiling professions. Doctors were in the bad news business. They nodded gravely and spoke in reassuring, largely incomprehensible medical jargon that allowed you to think, for a brief, blissful moment, that the illness, injury, or death to which they were referring was in some textbook—instead of in your family. What was this guy trying to sell me?

"It's called Fraxel," the plastic surgeon said in his infomercial voice. "Fraxel is a brand-new cosmetic treatment, the laser equivalent of fine sandpaper. We will use it to subtly smooth out the scar on your son's nose while stimulating the growth of new skin. Recovery is practically painless. Like having a mild sunburn."

"Sounds too good to be true," I said.

"We've had some great results," he said, flashing me his buffed incisors again.

I looked over at Sam. One nurse was playing with the blue surgical dye they used to mark the treatment area on his nose, dabbing some on her nose to make him laugh, while the other nurse tickled him to get him to hand over his baseball cards. They were about to point a *laser* at his face—why were they treating this like Romper Room?

Then everything started moving too fast. The doctor and the nurses closed in, a wall of surgical green between Sam and me. Maybe it was just the lights, but all of a sudden the room felt hot. I'd seen this all before. I flashed back to the night they stitched Sam up in the ER . . . the night they performed emergency surgery on Benny when he was in intensive care . . . the night my mother died . . .

The laser flashed. Sam cried out. And then it was all over.

They put a cold pack on Sam's nose, and he went back to winning the World Series as if nothing had happened.

I was stunned, literally. My legs went all jelly on me. The color drained from the room, everything fading to the milky white of the doctor's teeth. Except he wasn't smiling anymore.

"Get him on the table!"

They whisked Sam out of the room and laid me down on the operating table.

"Heeeeyy I'm ffffine . . . " I said, my mouth not working right as the room faded to a dot, a light at the end of a very long tunnel. Then the smelling salts grabbed me by the nose and hauled me back to the world.

"What the hell happened to me?" I asked the nurse as soon as I could get my mouth working again.

"You just fainted."

Fainted. When Sam needed me to be strong for him. *Fainted.* If it were physically possible to die of embarrassment, I would be pushing up daisies as we speak.

"It's perfectly natural. Many parents just become overwhelmed by seeing their children in pain. But he's okay now," she said.

"Are you sure?"

She nodded. "He's a great kid," she said, handing me a Kleenex.

That's when I noticed I was crying.

"He's okay . . . he's okay . . . he's okay . . . " I said it over and over again to make myself believe it. And then I broke down, in front of the nurse, a stranger, in a way that I had never allowed myself to in front of Rose and the boys during the entirety of our crisis. I told myself they needed me to be strong, to fight for them. And I wasn't wrong about that. Rose and I won the war but now we were losing the peace, losing each other.

Dad said I would know what to do when the time came, but what if the time had already come and gone?

THE TIME CAME FOR US, as it does for most, when we least expected it.

On a routine Sunday after the paper had been read but before the breakfast dishes had been done. It was just a moment, but it seemed to last a lifetime—perhaps because the rest of our lives hung in the balance.

Tachypsychia is the scientific term for those moments in life when time appears to stand still. In this state of heightened awareness—whether experienced by a soldier in combat, a star athlete "in the zone," or an average person in a traffic accident—our thinking speeds up so much that time, as we perceive it, actually slows down. This is what makes it possible to hit a major league fastball.

Or to have your entire life flash before you in an instant.

It was in the cards. The baseball cards. Sam had left them out in a diamond on the floor, abandoned his Miracle Mets for some other toy more shiny and new. Rose spied them there, forgotten, her '86 originals left for the dog to pee on, and she lost it.

"If things that I work so hard for are just going to be stepped on, what's the point of anything that I do? I'll just leave!"

She wasn't really yelling at Sam. She was yelling at the world. It's just that Sam was there to hear her.

"I'll—just—leave . . . "

Time stopped for me when I heard those words.

Rose's threat almost physically hung in the air. Everything but these words and the exact position of each member of my family receded from my mind. Light from the TV flickered on Benny's face as he sat on the couch in the living room. Rose stood in the dining room angrily pointing at the cards on the floor; breakfast dishes were still on the table. Sam stood six feet to her left clutching his new Game Boy. I was eight feet away in the kitchen holding a hot cup of coffee that I barely remembered pouring.

"I'll—just—leave . . . "

Rose had said these words to me before, many times, in moments of complete frustration—but never to Sam. She said these words without thinking, but unfortunately Sam was now too old to hear things like this and think Mommy just meant going to the store. The subtle outlines of his thunderbolt scar became pronounced, his face contracted into a mask of fear.

Behind this moment, so many other moments: I looked at Sam cringing before me and saw myself as a frightened boy, bobbing up and down in a sea of adult unhappiness. I couldn't look at Rose and not see my mother screaming on the balcony when I was fourteen. But I couldn't blame Rose for falling apart—that was probably the only sane response to everything we'd been through. It was only a matter of time and, on that given Sunday, the time had most definitely come.

What the hell do I do?

Dad said when the time came, I would know what to do. I knew what *he* would do. He would let things cool off, go for a walk, and hope for the best. For all the times in my life when he wasn't there, I could now forgive him because man-oh-man did I want to disappear right then, sink into the floor, become a piece of furniture, anything not to have to field this white hot potato of a moment that seemed to last forever.

"I'll—just—leave . . . "

I saw Benny turn his head in slow motion, as if the sound from Rose's outburst had, just that moment, arrived in the living room. He stared at me, big blue eyes unblinking, and I stared back at him. I remembered watching over him all those days and nights in the NICU—wondering if he was going to die, afraid to breathe, dying myself a little in the eternity between his every breath as I wondered if it would be his last. I did not sleep for those four days because I knew that death was close to him and I dared not let myself get caught napping.

Death was close to us now.

The slow kind, the kind that takes away a little piece of you every day you're afraid to be alive; afraid that life will hurt, that you will lose, that things will not work out. But it was death, just the same.

I knew him. I had spent too much time in Intensive Care Units, in emergency rooms, in the unending hell of little moments like this not to recognize him now.

"When the time comes, you will know what to do."

Rose retreated to the master bedroom. I followed her inside and closed the door.

"You need help," I said.

"What about *you*?"

"I need help, too."

"I'm tired of arguing with you about this!" she said, opening up her laptop. I took it from her.

"Give me back my laptop! It's not fair to jump me like this!"

Death didn't fight fair, so neither would I.

"I'm not arguing with you anymore. I'm *telling* you. Either you agree to get help, or I will leave you and I will take the kids."

Her head snapped back as if she'd been struck. She stared me down and I stared back.

Ultimatums are like true love—you have to mean it.

I did, and she knew it. This was either the end or a new beginning.

"But I love you," Rose said, her face now wet with tears.

"I love you, too. And that's why I'm not going to stand by you if it just means watching you fall apart. I grew up with a mom who went nuts and a dad who went to the office. That's going to be us if we don't get help. I'd rather lose you than live like that, so I need you to decide."

Rose turned away from me, shaking her head.

The Rose I married wouldn't have had to think about this. That Rose was fearless. Indomitable. Spontaneous. It was her love of life that made me love her, that made her the most beautiful woman I'd ever seen, lit from within by hidden candles that I thought could never blow out.

But maybe she wasn't that Rose anymore.

All the little moments we'd shared had done more than just pass through the hourglass. Time and pressure had worked on us. Worn us down.

Just as I was starting to give up hope, Rose extended her hand to me, shyly, like we were meeting for the first time, and, in a way, we were.

EPILOGUE: IKEA

ROSE, SAM, BENNY, and I have made it through many tough times together, but perhaps the truest test of the family unit is whether you can go to Ikea on a holiday sale weekend and not want to kill each other.

"I am sick of you projecting all of your mother issues onto me!"

"Save it for your therapist, okay? I'm just trying to raise a healthy kid!"

"And I'm not?"

"Well, if you didn't shove an f-ing Pop-Tart in his f-ing pie hole every time he went boo-hoo, maybe he wouldn't be so f-ing fat!"

The mother at the table next to ours in the Ikea cafeteria covered Junior's ears with her hands and said, "F-word you! That is a NO THANK YOU, Daddy! No thank you!"

Rose and I watched this little domestic drama play out at the table next to ours in the Ikea cafeteria and tried not to laugh.

"What's funny?" Sam asked.

"Funny? Ah . . . nothing, pal. Nothing's funny," I said, raising my glass of Ikea's special lingonberry juice to my mouth to hide my smile.

"Funny!" Benny said in his loud, clear voice. We sure got our money's worth on his speech therapy—now you couldn't get him to *stop* talking. "FUNNY!"

"Benny, shhh," Rose said, glancing at the family at the next table. I looked over at the father, fretting over his dog-eared Ikea catalogue.

"F—! We forgot the DRAG for the PAX!" he said.

"The *what* for the *what*?" his wife asked.

"The handle thingy for the wardrobe. Now we're going to have to go all the way back to storage solutions!"

I felt for the guy. This was a bad day for him. But the real tragedy of this man's life (based on the five minutes in which I sat in judgment) was this: If having to backtrack to storage solutions constituted a bad day, then the rest of his life was just going to be filled with bad days.

The good thing about living through a year from hell is that the rest of your life is pretty much heaven by comparison. Even when it looks like you're going to spend the rest of your life in therapy. Rose and I were now working, both individually and as a couple, to look closely enough at our difficult past to truly put it behind us. It was going to be a long journey, but at least we'd made the first step.

The Blue Beckham Bomber whisked us home from Ikea that day. Rose and I looked back at Sam and Benny napping in the backseat. There is nothing more beautiful in this world to me than the faces of my children, happy and at peace. Rose and I smiled. Our hands found each other.

"Thanks for not giving up on me," Rose said.

I squeezed her hand tight, wanting to believe that this moment of accidental loveliness would last forever, that the road ahead would always be smooth, the wind always at our backs. But if life has taught me anything of a certainty, it's that nothing is certain. That didn't make the happy accident of us holding hands that Ikea afternoon any less lovely. For me, only more so. Happiness, like all precious things, is valuable because it's rare.

So I would hold on to this moment and hold on to this good woman's hand for just as long as life allowed.

ACKNOWLEDGMENTS

I NEED TO THANK a long list of people who were good enough to mistake me for a writer early and often enough to afford me the opportunity to write this book.

First, I've got to give it up for everybody there at the mother ship, Rodale, starting with the President and Chief Executive Officer, Steven Pleshette Murphy. How the guy finds time to offer counsel and encouragement to a mere scribbler such as myself, miles down the corporate ladder from his lofty perch atop this kick-ass company, is beyond me, but I'm deeply grateful. It is my honor and privilege to kiss the ring of Karen Rinaldi, Senior Vice President, General Manager, Publishing Director, and Overall Vixen of Rodale Books, and offer heartfelt thanks to my editor, Shannon Welch, for her tireless acumen in helping shape the final manuscript of this book. Also want to give a big shout-out to outgoing Rodale vixens Liz Perl and especially Leigh Haber, for rolling the dice on the cockeyed proposition that a failed screenwriter and fledgling humor columnist at *Men's Health* magazine might have an honest-to-goodness memoir in him. And speaking of *Men's Health* magazine, mucho, mucho gracias to Editor-in-Chief/*Übermensch* David Zinczenko for giving me my break there and especially to Executive Editor Bill Phillips for being my good friend and for helping turn my illegible, inchoate rants into well-written universal takeaways about life.

Life as I know it would be impossible without the existence of my great friends and co-founders of the Barnaby Googe Society, the writers and editrixes nonpareil Andrea Chapin and Patricia McCormick. Deepest thanks to them both for all the editorial advice (they're really smart that way) and "chicken soup for the soul" that went into the writing of this book. Also want to offer profound thanks to my agent and an honorary member of the Barnaby Googe Society, Sally Wofford-Girand, for her friendship and indefatigable championing of my work.

And, finally, I am most grateful for my family. I want to thank my boys for inspiring and humbling me on a daily basis. There is no greater honor in life than getting to be your dad. And speaking of dads, you can't do much better than mine. Deepest thanks to my Pop—not only for taking this journey with me but also for giving me leave to write about it so candidly. And, saving the best for last, I am so grateful to my wife—for all the years, for all her belief in me, for our two beautiful boys, for everything.